Order no.
27879

CHANGING PA

AN AUTOBIOGRAPHY

NORMAN DUNKLEY

WITHDRAWN FROM
PLYMOUTH LIBRARY SERVICES

EYELEVEL

First published in Great Britain by
Eyelevel Books 1998

Copyright © Norman Dunkley 1998

The Author asserts the moral right to
be identified as the author of this work

ISBN 1 902528 00 X

Printed in England by
Biddles Limited
Guildford and King's Lynn

All rights reserved. No part of this publication may be
reproduced, stored in a retrieval system, or transmitted,
in any form or by any means, electronic, mechanical,
photocopying, recording or otherwise, without the prior
permission of the author.

Dedicated to my wife Margaret

—·+●+·—

"Not what I gain,
But what I give
Measures the worth
Of the life I live."

RED			
CRO			
PT	12/98		
PK			

Acknowledgements

My grateful thanks go to my brother, Bruce, for his help with regard to the period 1927 to 1950, and to my son, John, for his help with the compilation.

My thanks must also go to cousin Peter for the family tree and information gleaned from the Devon County Census and Records Office, for family dates and photos and other information.

To Plympton St. Maurice Civic Association and references I have made to the "History of Plympton Erle".

To Jon Moore and Jacqueline Hollis, with whose help I am able to publish this manuscript.

Norman Dunkley
Worcester 1998

PART ONE

1927 - 1956

*Father in Australian Imperial Forces uniform,
probably around 1915*

Chapter One

My Family

My Father, Herbert John Dunkley

He was born on 10th May 1892 in Queen Charlotte's Hospital, Marylebone Road, London. His home address was No. 13, Gray's Inn Place, Pimlico, and he was christened Herbert John after his father, described as a warehouseman at an ironmonger's. His mother was Rosina Rosalind Dunkley, nee Bowden, of St. George's. She died at Upper Rathbone Place of phthisis exhaustion on 24th February 1904, aged 34. His father died sometime during the Second World War (1939-1945) from natural causes.

Father emigrated to Australia in 1912 and he got employment as a stockman in the outback at first. He was later described as a cook on his marriage certificate (in 1915) and later still, as provision merchant on my brother Bruce's birth certificate in 1923.

On his marriage certificate and Bruce's birth certificate, he added the name Ronald to his Christian names and gave his place of birth as the Isle of Bute, Scotland. There seems no logical reason for this, because he was born in London. He also showed his father's occupation as upholsterer on his marriage certificate.

left; Mother and father,
wedding day
December, 1915
below; family group 1924.
Seated is Ronald, with
Bruce on mother's knee.
opposite; mother,
around 1905

My Mother, Nellie Winifred Collier

She was born on 10th January 1888 at her home in Yealm Bridge Cottage, Yealmpton, South Devon, the second child of six children. Her father was Frederick Joseph Collier, described as a master gardener. Her mother was called Ellen Mary Collier, nee Scholar, who was of Cornish descent.

Mother went into domestic service after leaving school and at first worked in a large house in Ottery St. Mary, and later at Broadclyst with her sister Ada, who married Claud Johnson, before she herself emigrated to Australia in 1913 with her cousin, Bessie.

Both my parents emigrated to Australia, Father in 1912 and Mother in 1913. Mother eventually got a job as a cook on a sheep farm near a town called Ballina in Queensland. Father joined the farm as a farmhand and that is where they met. The marriage took place on 15th December 1915 at St. Andrew's Anglican Church in Lismore, New South Wales, and it was witnessed by her brother Harold, who had already emigrated to Australia before her after his marriage in 1912.

Frank, 1951

Ronald, 1945

Bruce, Singapore, 1946

Norman, July 1950

My maternal grandmother was not expected to live so it was Mother's wish to see her before she died. They arrived in England on 28th October 1924 with Ron and Bruce. Mother at that time was six months pregnant. They arrived in Plymouth and went first to live at Forder Gardens, where my maternal grandparents were living. Forder Gardens were situated on Dartmoor between Bovey Tracey and Princetown. They then went to live in Moorland Avenue, Plympton, to await the birth of their third child.

My Brother Ronald

He was born on 18th February 1921 in Lismore, New South Wales, and he was christened Ronald Frederick, presumably after Father and our maternal grandfather.

My Brother Bruce

He was born on 2nd July 1923 at Kerr Street, Ballina, New South Wales. He was christened Bruce (don't know why) and William after Mother's youngest brother.

My Brother Frank

He was born on 19th February 1925 at Moorland Avenue, Plympton, and he was christened Francis Herbert after Aunt Susie's first husband, Frank Windsor, and Father.

Father, having set up a shop in one room known as Castle Stores at the Old Castle Inn in the parish of St. Maurice, Plympton, opposite the church in the later part of 1925.

Frank emigrated to Rhodesia in 1954 with his wife and son and died from leukæmia in October 1972 aged 47 years.

My birth

I was born in the room which was the original shop on 3rd March 1927 and, according to my Mother, I was two weeks late in arriving. I was christened on Palm Sunday Norman Maurice, there being no family connections with my names. I have always believed that, as the view from that room was of the old Norman castle remains and the church of St. Maurice, I was given those two names.

Grandmother and Grandfather, probably around 1920
opposite; Grandmother at about the same time

My maternal grandfather, Frederick Joseph Collier

Grandfather lived at Forder Gardens, a nursery and market garden, with my grandmother and their six children, having moved there from Yealmpton in 1900. When I was about eight weeks old Mother spent quite some time there that summer with me and my brother Frank. Grandfather went to market each week to Newton Abbot to sell his produce and eventually, in about 1930, he sold the business and bought a smaller nursery in Kingskerswell, where he lived until 1947, when he died at the age of 90 years.

Grandmother, Ellen Mary Scholar, had died at Forder Gardens in November 1925 at the age of 69 years. They are buried together in the churchyard in Bovey Tracey.

FREDERICK JOSEPH COLLIER
b. 1855 d. 1947

MARY ADA
b.
d.

CLAUDE JOHNSON
b.
d.

m 1911?

NELLIE WINIFRED
b. 10/1/1888
d. 22/12/1977

HERBERT JOHN DUNKLEY
b. 10/5/1892
d. 28/2/1960

m

BERNARD CLAUDE
b.
d. 7/7/1981

m

MOLLY
b.
d.

WINIFRED MARY
b. 8/6/1912
d. 19/8/1995

E. MORETON
b.
d. 11/11/1990

m

JULIE
b. 28/4/1938

CHRISTOPHER
b. 1946

RONALD FREDERICK
b. 18/2/1921
d.

M. Plympton

JOYCE
b. 1/9/1920
d. 4/11/1994

BRUCE WILLIAM
b. 2/7/1923
d.

m 1947

CELIA
b. 9/3/1920
d.

FRANCIS HERBERT
b. 19/2/1925
d. 25/10/1972

JANET
b. 11/5/1949

ALLAN BRUCE
b. 16/11/1948
d. 3/1/1975

STEPHEN RUSSEL
b. 13.4.1950

Extract from the family tree of
Norman Maurice Dunkley

LINDA ANN
b. 20/11/1952

ROBERT EDWARD WEBB
b. 7/10/1945

m 12/11/1977

JAMES ROBERT
b. 13/7/1981

SARAH LOUISE
b. 8/6/1983

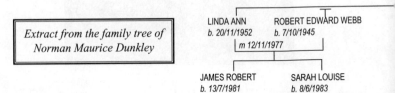

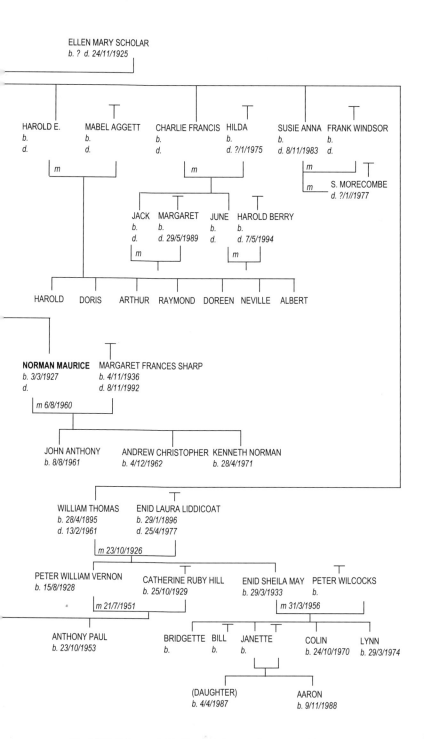

Chapter Two

MY HOME &
HOME LIFE

From the time that I was born we lived in this one room until 1932. There was a kitchen which was behind the shop and it was dark, having only one gas lamp to see by at night, a door led outside to the back to a water tap on the left. To the right was an area which served as a storeroom, and the outside lavatory was further outside in the back garden. At first, a candle was used to see by to get to it at night and if it went out, you had to grope your way back in the dark. Later on we used a pocket torch. Across the garden opposite the lavatory there were the remains of an old skittle alley, and also outside opposite the backdoor, there was a copper boiler for getting the washing done. To do this, Mother had to light a coal fire to bring the water up to boiling point; she would light the fire at 6.00 a.m. each Monday.

Saturday night was a real ritual bath of the week event in a galvanised bath tub in front of the coal fire. I always went first, followed by my brother Frank. After his bath, the water was changed and my other two brothers took it in turn, first Bruce, then Ron, he being the eldest.

By then, it was 9.00 p.m. and sometimes, if I was not asleep, I had the cane across my legs. (Later, we all worked out a dodge from the cane - as it hit the bedclothes we would pull the sheet up tight and bend our legs and shout as if in pain at the same time). Father, to my knowledge, did not help Mother with changing the water. He just sat and watched or went out to his club. I do not know how they managed to have a bath themselves. Being two adults and four children living in these primitive conditions and squalor must have been unbearable. In 1932, two bedrooms were built over the shop and the staircase leading to them was built at one end of the kitchen. This improved the situation by making the bedroom/sitting room just a sitting room, but we still ate our meals there.

One thing Father had brought home from Australia was a concertina and he sat on the firebox by the fire and played it in the evenings. However, it was not long before he stopped playing it. Someone he knew was interested in it so he sold it to him.

Our cousin, Winifred, whom we called "Girlie" (why, I don't know), very often came to visit us when she was training to be a nurse, and because I was not fond of cabbage at that time, she was given the task of force feeding me with it whenever we had it. It put me off certain kinds of cabbage for many years after that.

One night I called out to Mother that I wanted the pot and in the dark (we still only had gas lights), she missed her bearings and fell down the stairs and broke her arm. Later on, in 1934, Father persuaded the landlord (a Mr. Scoble) to build a bathroom at the rear of the shop and this meant no more going to the loo at the back of the garden in all weathers all year round. I hated going out in pitch darkness.

Father decided that with two bedrooms and a bathroom, he had to have the gas lights replaced by having electricity installed. This was a great improvement to the rooms that we lived in and it was quite a novelty at first until we got used to it. The new bathroom was fitted with a bath, hand basin and toilet. Fitted over the bath was a gas geyser to heat the water. We used to turn the gas on and let it build up before turning the pilot light towards the gas jets. This would then create a mini explosion which shook the bathroom. A mirror was hung on one wall and Mother's old wash stand with a marble top was placed under it.

Father also got the builders to line one shop wall with sheets of tin on a wooden frame. He had been plagued with mice from next door but this lining with the sheets of tin put a stop to that.

Father treated me in the same way as my brothers in that if

and when we did anything wrong, we were severely punished. My disability made no difference to him and he often used to hit me, especially across the back of my legs. Mother, on the other hand, was a more gentle person and not as strict, unlike Father, and could and did see the other person's point of view in most things. She was very much more approachable than he was, but there were times when she could be as strict as he was, but not so often. To Father's annoyance, she often agreed with us in a dispute if we were right, but Father could never see our side of things. Within the family he liked to think that his word was law, and that he was always right. He was a person who tried to impress the world outside the home that he was a good family man who was eventually to serve many years on the Parochial Church and Parish Councils, and later the Rural District Council. He did do quite a lot of good for the parish; re-housing families from the slum area after the council houses were built was one thing he was noted for, but we at home suffered by coming a poor second to many things because of it.

After the shop closed, he went out every evening leaving Mother on her own to cope with putting us to bed. He said he needed to go out because he had been in the shop all day. What about Mother? She never did go out, only perhaps to get her hair permed once a year, or to go to the library some afternoons, and at very infrequent times, to take some of us, if not all, to Plymouth to buy new clothes.

* * * *

Due to my disability it took me nearly two years before I could walk; my parents did not worry about this until it was noticed that my right foot was pointing towards the centre of my left one. It was not until 1932 that any positive action was taken when it was suggested by the GP that I should go to a hospital in Plymouth to see an orthopædic surgeon. His diagnosis was, firstly, that he did not know the true cause of the deformity, but his findings were on the assumption that I had poliomyelitis in my right leg (known then as infantile paralysis), because my leg below the knee had not developed normally - it was about 1¼ inches shorter than my left leg overall.

Throughout most of my life I have been an out-patient at many hospitals in different parts of the country and I have had many operations on my leg since 1935. Until the age of 19 I had to wear a leg iron which came up to just below the knee with a built-up boot to compensate for the leg's shortness. Later, when I was 50 I wore another iron for a year. Wearing such an iron caused many problems such as sores below the knee and abrasions near the ankle from the 'T' strap. At night I had to wear a tin night shoe which was even more intolerable. It was lined with cotton wool and held in place by a 2 inch wide bandage and had sharp edges which tore the sheets. This made sleeping in a double bed with my brother, Frank, very uncomfortable for him as well as myself, and caused a few arguments between us. Naturally I got the blame for starting them. In later years, when I had to have a new iron (calliper), the cost had risen from two shillings and sixpence to five shillings. Father, at first, refused to pay the increase and that was the first time that I heard the words 'rising costs' and the expression "the cost of materials had gone up".

Looking back, this immobilising of my right ankle and foot was the worst thing that could have been done for my treatment. I now believe that had I been given normal usage of my leg, it would have got stronger and developed a great deal more and not be as weak as it has been all my life. But I expect in those days very little was known about polio and its treatment, hence the immobilisation.

It was decided early in the year of 1935 that I needed surgery to stop my right foot pointing inwards. Father enquired how this was to be paid for. He was advised to join the 'Penny in the Pound Scheme', costing, to start with, three shillings every quarter. (This amount increased over the years to six shillings and eight pence until the introduction of the National Health Service in 1948). In September, I was admitted to the Green Bank Hospital in Plymouth for the first of many operations to my foot.

In those days chloroform was used to put you to sleep and for many days after the operation I felt really ill trying to get it out of my system. I then developed tonsillitis which further delayed my discharge from hospital, the operation being successful. After a month I left the hospital; Father had ordered a private hire car to bring us home. The driver was Harry Olver who had always taken an interest in my well-being and he never forgot to ask about me whenever he saw my parents or myself.

He did not drive me home direct but by a different route so that I had a longer ride in the car. My leg was in Plaster of Paris for a further month to six weeks and I lost quite a lot of time from school. No attempt was made by the school authorities to give me extra tuition while I was at home. I had missed quite a lot and in consequence, my subjects suffered so much, especially my mathematics, that I was well down in my class of thirty-five pupils in my exams.

In 1938, Father became a Freemason and when he took me to see the orthopaedic surgeon shortly after joining, the surgeon suggested that as he was now "One of Them", he could send me to the Royal Masonic Hospital in London for further treatment. Father replied that he did not join for charity. It was pointed out to him that I would be treated by the best medical team in the country, but he still said, "No".

Over the years, I held a grudge against Father because I did not understand why he said no, until it was pointed out to me many years later that Mother would have had to go with me which would have cost Father a lot of money for her lodgings etc.. It was a golden opportunity that was missed, and had Father had the means to send me, who knows my leg might have developed quite differently. It was another two years before I began to go on my own for these check-ups, but still I had to give a full account to Father on my return of what was said.

The surgeon would not make much comment to me other than the foot and leg had not got any worse and to come back in six months' time. So there was not much that I could tell Father.

Chapter Three

PLYMPTON ERLE

The ancient town of Plympton Erle, as it was first called in Norman times, can be dated back to the year 904 and was a borough town with the River Plym flowing down from Dartmoor on its north west side when what is now Plymouth was a down with sheep grazing, dividing the Rivers Plym and Tamar. The River Tamar divides Devon from Cornwall. As children, we learnt a rhyme which went as follows:

> *"When Plympton was a Borough Town,*
> *Plymouth was a fuzzy down"*

On the corner of George Lane and Long Cause Street is Plympton House, designed by Sir Christopher Wren. It is now known as St. Peter's Convent and is in use as a nursing home. From the parish it was only a matter of about a ten minute walk to reach the countryside and lanes, where it was peaceful. You could see the farm animals grazing in the various fields, which belonged to the local farmers.

Some of the lanes had their own names such as Cherry Park Lane, Six O'clock Lane, Backside Lane; then there was Ridge Road and Bullars Hill, named after General Redvers Bullar of Boer War fame.

The fields were bordered by typical Devon high hedges

which had all kinds of wild flowers growing and wild animals living in them. They were a very good habitat for birds to nest in as well as for wild fruit like strawberries and elderberries, which could be gathered during the summer months. There were also two coppices and a wood that we could pick wild flowers from; in the wood were a few eating chestnut trees. In some hedges trees had been planted in them at intervals along the lanes.

In the distance the church tower could be seen and you could hear the bells very clearly when they were being rung.

One field was set aside and a cemetery was created at the beginning of Cherry Park Lane.

From 1934 a row of council houses was built in the field along one side of the road called Long Cause. These were occupied by the parishioners who had large families. They were living in very bad, overcrowded conditions in the cottages and shared an outside toilet, there being no bathrooms.

In Fore Street the pavement on one side was in parts higher than the rest of the street. This was because the pent houses on that side had an upstairs room that was built over and in line with the outside edge of the pavement, supported by two feet thick stone pillars. Further down Fore Street was the ancient Guildhall where the parish council held their monthly meetings. Along its walls were hung paintings of local dignitaries as well as the "Age of Innocence" by Sir Joshua Reynolds, which was presented to the parish in the mid-nineteen thirties.

The main hall was hired for various functions by clubs and other associations to hold dances, dinners, concerts, and the annual spring flower show. The scholars of the local primary St. Maurice School, in School Lane, would entertain with a concert before the prizes were given out to the various winners who attended the show in the evening along with the other parishioners.

Next to the Guildhall is the old fire engine house. The horse-drawn fire engine is a museum piece and is now housed in the new fire station in Glen Road.

The Castle Green was used for games and recreation and in the summer it was rented out to two different fairs and circuses each year. I remember Father telling us one year that a fixed rate from the fair owners was one penny per wheel a day, but the rent for the circus was different.

At its east end were the Castle Rock remains from which you have panoramic views of the area. The Rock, which was curved in a semicircle built on a mound, had three sections with holes in the centre about two feet square. When we were very small we could crawl through each one. The longest one was higher at its centre and if you were too big, you could get stuck in the middle if you were not careful. My brother Frank did get stuck and it took some time for him to get out; I don't think he ever went into it again. There was a flag pole erected to celebrate Queen Victoria's Jubilee. On festival and saints' days and for funerals the Union Jack was always flown. The flag pole has since been removed.

A moat used to surround the Castle Green, the water coming from the River Plym which was tidal at that time, when it was first built. At its west end there is a very large house called Castle Barbican which was used as a Grammar School from 1921 until about 1937, when a new school was built about two miles away in the other parish of St. Mary.

The parish of St. Mary was named after the church but it only dates from the sixteenth century. Prior to that it was part of the River Plym and was mostly marsh land.

The Norman church of St. Maurice was founded in the 12th Century and was first named after Thomas à Becket; either side of the high altar there is a large painting of both men, St. Maurice on the right side of the altar and Thomas à Becket on the left. To the right of the high altar is the Lady Chapel which stands on the original site of the Church. I believe there are only five other churches named after St. Maurice in the country.

The carved wooden rood screen that stretches across the church from the north side to the south divides the chancel from the nave, and was built without nails, held together solely by wooden dowels; it has lasted for many centuries.

Centred on the top, also carved in wood, is Christ Crucified with Mary and Joseph on either side. This carved screen is worth a visit because of the detailed work done by skilled craftsmen from a bygone age. The south wall has a war memorial in honour of the fallen in the Great War of 1914-1918, and of World War Two 1939-1945. At the west end the tower has a fine peal of eight bells which were recast in 1936 and re-hung in 1937. On the north side of the church there is a marble profile memorial of Sir Joshua Reynolds, the well-known portrait painter, who was born in Plympton Erle in 1723. Later, he became the first President of the Royal Academy of Art in London, and he was Knighted by George III. He was a pupil of the Grammar School when his father was the headmaster in the 18th Century. In the churchyard there is an epitaph which reads as follows:

"Here layeth ye offspring of Will'm and Jane Dodridge
who died between June ye 1st 1733
and March ye 1st 1742.
Beneath this place are in line,
Brothers and sisters number nine,
Who were cropt off in blooming years
Which caused their parents many tears,
But cease to mourn good parents dear.
We are not lost but sleeping here.
Till judgement day when Christ doth call,
In Heav'n we trust you'll meet us all."

Outside in George Lane, to the south east of the church on the boundary wall of the original Grammar School, is a commemorative stone plaque in Sir Joshua's honour with details of his birth and death and being made the first President of the Royal Academy of Art. He made many visits to his birthplace in his lifetime and he became Mayor in 1773. The Grammar School was also famous for its education of Northcote, Haydon and Eastlake, three more famous painters in the history of painting of that Century. The Grammar School was still in use as part of the school until 1933. It was then used as a branch of the County Library for several years and it is now a listed building.

The new Grammar School was opened in 1937 in Seymour Road and there were three house names of Reynolds, Northcote and Hayden, after famous scholars of the 18th Century.

Sir Joshua was also a great friend of Robert Adam who had a country house at Marsh Mills known as Saltram House, and he had also painted two children of the Parker family, with whom he was friendly.

Before joining the choir I always went to evensong on Sundays in order to avoid going to bed at 6.00 p.m. summer or winter, my parents, especially Father, having in mind that we had to get up for school the next morning. In the summer of 1936, at the age of nine, I became a probationer in the church choir and a full member in early December, following in my brothers' footsteps. That was the first time in the church's history that there were four brothers in the choir at the same time. Every August, our rector went away on retreat or a holiday and his place was taken by a very old rector. We were led to believe he was shell shocked in the First World War because he would shake quite a lot, especially his hands. We nicknamed him "Johnny Dewdrop" because each time when he gave a sermon, his nose would drip fluid over the pulpit. There were about sixteen boys and ten men in the choir and sometimes choirboys were not the angelic lads they purported to be. For instance, one choir man always arrived at 6.29 p.m. for evensong. More than once his cassock sleeve was tied in a knot and this delayed the start of the service by five minutes.

It was about two years before that Wally Hayman and I became good friends. He started as a server in church and took up bell ringing as well. Besides this he was responsible for putting the hymn and psalm numbers up on the boards for each service every Sunday. Eventually, I got involved with these duties which also included setting out the music for the choir for evensong.

After lunch we went for three hourly walks which usually meant at least three to four miles on average, two outward and two back. One of our favourite walks was to Sherford Limekiln ruins where we looked for white violets in the hedgerows in the springtime. In summer, we would return home the long way through Elburton and pass the vineries. Several acres were covered in greenhouses which specialised in growing many varieties of tomatoes, cucumbers and lettuces. Further along that lane towards Plympton wild strawberries could be gathered from the hedges in June.

Then, after evensong, we would walk three miles to a pub called The Miners Arms for a drink and a pasty made in the pub kitchen. They were well worth all that walking. They were hot, just out of the oven. Sometimes we had to wait for them to finish cooking; they cost 9d each. We would normally discuss how each service went each week and whether or not the choir did justice to the hymns, especially at festival times such as Christmas and Easter. This was a weekly event until Wally went to Bath to work at the Admiralty in his early twenties.

I also became a server like my brothers and Wally before me and so this made me more involved than ever with attending the church services. Wally and I often served together from then on. In the summer we had a choir outing, mostly to seaside towns, and early in the New Year we had our Christmas party.

Chapter Four

SCHOOLS & LEISURE

From the age of five we were made to go to Sunday School each Sunday afternoon until we reached the age of eleven. One of the teachers was called Miss Connie Dyer who taught my brothers and me in turn. She had a warbling voice when she sang, so when we were in Church, we tried not to sit next to or near her because we would get a fit of the giggles hearing her warbling. Then, at the age of eleven, we went on to Bible Class. We were awarded a Bible and Prayer Book for each year's full attendance and what we had learnt. This was usually followed by confirmation classes to be confirmed at the age of thirteen.

These classes were held at the Rectory and each of us in turn was supposed to be given a pep talk by the Rector when nearing confirmation day. The Rector asked me to get a large piece of paper and write all my sins down and he would hear my confessions the following Thursday at 7.00 p.m.. At the appointed time, I walked past the Rectory and went to see my friend Wally. He told me that all the group had been asked to do the same, and we all took the same action. We were C. of E. and not Catholics. Later, we realised that the Rev. Herbert Ernest Bennett was Anglo-Catholic. Anyway, who at the age of thirteen had, if any, sins to confess in those days? We were never asked by the Rector why we had not turned up and, of course, most parents were unaware of this request by him.

At all the festivals throughout the year we were expected to attend so as to be eligible to go to the summer outing or Christmas party, and to get a Sunday School or Bible Class prize.

My school years were not very happy. The infants school was all right and both teachers were very kind but firm in their teaching. There were about 25 children to each class. We had a coal fire in the classroom in the winter and our coats were hung around the guard to get them dry and warm before going out to play and when leaving for home. In the summer months, sometimes the teacher would take us to play games on the old Castle Green.

In 1934 the first ten council houses were completed in Longcause and so ten families were moved out of the bad houses that they were in. Many of my school friends moved to these houses including the Lowden family and Roy West and his family. Ida Lowden at first did not like walking home on her own from school, so I was picked by the teacher to walk home with her.

When I was due to go to the Junior School in September 1934 at the age of seven, the head teacher held me back from going because I would have to cross the busy main road in Ridgeway to get to my next school. She was not prepared to take that risk with me and told my parents so. About a month after the term had started the school inspector paid a visit to the school and saw me still there. Although he understood the teacher's reasons for holding me back, he said it was wrong and I must move on to the junior school at half term.

By the teacher's action in not sending me to the junior school at the beginning of term in September, I missed being taught how to write and I was told to "Copy off the blackboard, boy." That is why my handwriting is very poor, as I had only been taught to print at the infant school.

A few weeks after starting at the new junior school, the school health nurse arrived to check me for cleanliness. This included checking for head lice and an eye test. I was awarded a clean hands badge. I was sent home with a note signed by the nurse saying that I needed to wear glasses because my left eye was "lazy". She had referred me to the optician who was also in attendance and he confirmed her findings. I told both Father and Mother that I had also seen the optician but Father would not believe me, nor the result of the test.

Next morning, he went to the school and asked to see the nurse. She explained the condition of my eye to him but Father was not convinced and asked to see the optician, who explained yet again and verified that I needed glasses as the nurse had said. A pair of glasses, for which Father had to pay, were prescribed for me. When I got home from school that afternoon, he still accused me of "putting it on" and that my eye was all right and he said to Mother "How much more is he going to cost me?" How wrong he was! I have worn glasses ever since.

During the Advent period of 1937, I was chosen to play the third King for the school Nativity play and being a choir boy meant that I had to sing a solo verse of "We Three Kings". I was dressed up in a robe with a crown on my head (made by Mother and myself) and carried a casket with my gift in it. I only remember my Mother coming to the school to see me, Father having to work in the shop.

In late-January 1938, we all experienced a natural phenomenon known as "The Aurora Borealis". At first, we did not know what it was. The vivid cascades of coloured lights in the northern hemisphere were very brilliant, and some people quite thought that the end of the world had begun. Next day at school we were asked if we had seen the lights, and when we said "Yes", we were told it was possibly a once-in-a-lifetime experience.

In August, our summer holidays from school were curtailed to two weeks from four because we had to help in digging with picks and shovels for the air-raid shelters in the school grounds. They were dug out about six to seven feet deep and five feet wide and formed in a zigzag shape. The soil that was dug out was put across the top of the shelters to cover the roof of timbers. There was a crisis on at the time because the adults expected another war to start.

That September, I began in the senior school and with the threat of war as well as starting at a new school, I was feeling more apprehensive than normal. Quite frankly, I was frightened.

Soon after starting at the senior school, as was usual, the nurse duly arrived for her inspection of the new intake. Eventually, we all had to be examined for our general health and to make sure we were getting our milk each day. Again, my eyes were tested and it was decided to put a patch over my right eye to encourage the left one to do more work. As it happened, it was during the woodwork lesson that I was sent for, and on my return, the master could not resist calling me Nelson, which did not please me because all the other boys were laughing at the remark. The master saw that I was very upset to the point of crying and he came to me and apologised, saying it was only a joke. He was a very understanding master and from then on, I always got on well with him.

Unlike the science master, who also took me for P.E. This master took a dislike to me from the moment that he first saw me. He would have me up for ridicule in front of the class whenever he could, mainly because I was not allowed to take part in P.E. or games; but there was nothing that I could do about it.

Some of the teachers at this school always took a negative attitude where I was concerned because of my disability and three-monthly visits to hospital. They would not let me do any games or P.E., or swimming lessons in the summertime, because they would not take the responsibility if I had an accident, so I could only watch. On reflection, it was the wrong attitude because the best thing for me was exactly that: plenty of exercise, P.E. and games. This could be the reason why I never took any interest in sport except for snooker, billiards, and cricket in later life.

The only subjects that I did enjoy were history, geography and music. I liked to know where all the countries were and to know how the people lived, compared to our way of life. So geography was a very interesting subject for me at which I excelled, being always in the first three or four in the exams. As for music, I cannot read it but I can follow it and I have a good ear for tunes and harmonies. I was very good at quickly picking up a new tune or descants at school and in later years, the bass line in choral works in the youth choral club (more of that later). The history of this country was interesting, knowing how wars, crusades and the Royal Families of the past Centuries affect us now in the Twentieth Century.

One science lesson that I well remember was when the master was in a good mood. He was explaining the electric lighting and pointed out the lights in the classroom. He told us that when the War was over, it was quite possible that the lighting of the future would come from tubes and not bulbs, and that they would be fixed to the ceilings rather than be suspended as they were at the time. We were amazed to hear this, but as we now know, he was referring to fluorescent lighting which today we take for granted.

He was also responsible for showing films of the industries of this country from coal mines, iron and steel works to other heavy industries in the North of England. These black and white films depicted appalling working and living conditions from the 1920s and 1930s. The houses were built back-to-back with no indoor sanitation and the coal mines had pit ponies to pull the coal trucks with nothing but coal dust to breathe. Compared to the way we lived, we considered ourselves to be very lucky.

* * * *

In 1927 Father was the founder in setting up a young men's recreation club with a snooker table and tennis table. The idea was to keep youngsters off the streets and the club soon became very popular. Father taught the members how to play card games such ass whist and cribbage.

He was a fairly good snooker player as well and taught many a youngster how to play, including my brother Frank who, in later years, went on to win the snooker tournament in three consecutive years in the Plymouth and District League. He was a natural player and could win the majority of his games. The members became so good that, in a short space of time, they were able to enter the Plymouth and District League competitions for table tennis, billiards and snooker and won many cups and shields.

When I became a hospital out-patient in 1932, I was given a net stocking to collect money for the hospital towards the children's ward for Christmas. From then on, every December I was allowed to go to the club and pass the stocking around. If I got as much as five shillings in pennies and half-pennies, that would fill the stocking.

In 1930, when Bruce was seven years old, he had a ride in a trolley with about five other boys. A front wheel collapsed, the trolley spilled the boys out and Bruce suffered a green fracture of his arm.

During our formative years, the thing that we did not like was getting boils on our skin, or having chilblains. Frank had several boils but the one I remember most was the one Bruce had. This was in 1932, when he was nine years old. He developed a large boil on his back and it took Mother quite an effort to burst it. She was not prepared for what was to happen. On bursting, the pus spread all over his back and Mother wiped it off with a clean cloth. There was no form of antiseptic in the house to clean his back. A few days later Bruce's back became covered in a cluster of boils of various sizes and it was several weeks before his back was cleared of them.

I had chilblains on my feet during many winters until I reached the age for the senior school. They were often very itchy, so I used a cream to put on them called Zambuk which Father sold in the shop.

One treat allowed from the shop during my school days was a halfpenny worth of sweets (equal to one ounce) six days a week and on Sundays we were allowed one pennyworth (two ounces), but if you misbehaved, you went without as part of the punishment.

We knew a few characters while we were growing up. One person that comes to mind was a banjo player who came out from Plymouth always on a Thursday. He stood against the churchyard wall under the holly tree opposite the shop, singing and playing his banjo. He wore a beret on his head and he had a large goitre on his chin; his face was very red. The rumour went around that he owned several houses in Plymouth, but whether that was true or not, I never found out.

At the age of three, an outing I can remember was a 'bus ride into Plymouth with my parents and brothers to spend the afternoon on Plymouth Hoe watching the ships and pleasure boats sailing in the Sound. On this occasion, when it was time to start for home, as the weather was fine Father decided that we could walk home, a distance of five miles. Imagine the groans from my brothers. They had been running around and got tired and now they were expected to help to push me in turns in my pushchair on the way home. A few years later, I was expected to walk home with the rest of them, but my parents did take it in turns to carry me each time that I felt tired.

At the age of four I had a tricycle and the only way that I could ride it was by pushing with my feet on the ground, my right foot would not stay on the pedal.

One of our neighbours had an allotment and, from the age of six, I used to go with him after tea and come back later with a bunch of the original pinks called Mrs. Simpkins. They had a lovely perfume and I could not wait some years to get a bunch, which were always given to Mother. One year, he grew marrows and printed my name on one. We watched my name get bigger as the marrow grew. Mother had that as well. When he died, I could no longer go to that allotment and pick any more pinks, a great disappointment to me.

Mother was very knowledgeable at naming many wild flowers as well as the cultivated ones, and we all learnt quite a lot about them from her. No doubt she learnt quite a lot from her father, my grandfather Collier.

In those early days I also took scraps of vegetables and kitchen waste to another neighbour, Mrs. Curtis, who kept chickens, and I was always given one or two eggs laid that day; they made a lovely tea for me.

On Sundays, we had to wear our best suits because we had to look smart for attending the church services, and they were carefully brushed and pressed and put away by Mother on Mondays until the next Sunday morning. At home we had a gramophone which was not allowed to be played on a Sunday, as Mother felt that Sunday was a day for going to church. That was until the advent of our first wireless (radio) which I think arrived in 1935. It was a Cossor and it had an accumulator and high-tension batteries in the back, with very large valves. It cost sixpence to have the accumulator recharged each week and Frank and I mixed up the wires once and caused a valve to blow out. The programmes did not start until about 5.00 p.m. each day and you had a choice of two programmes - the Home Service or the Light Programme. At first, Mother did not think it correct to have entertainment on a Sunday, but she was outvoted and in the end resigned herself to the change.

One Saturday, when it was a very wet day we could not go out. So, in the afternoon, we went to the store and strung up lemonade bottles filled with different levels of water and tried to get a tune out of them; we succeeded in playing "The Bells of St. Mary's".

Also in 1935 we celebrated King George V's Jubilee. The day started with a carnival procession with prizes for the best float. Ron took several snaps with a camera and I think he won a prize for the results. Later in the day we were all given a mug with the King's and Queen's portrait on it (I still have mine). We had organised games such as a sack race, relay race, rounders, a cricket match, three-legged race etc., and there was ice cream for sale.

I remember one boy winning a pocket watch in the sack race, valued at two shillings and sixpence, which was a lot of money in those days to children of primary school age.

The day finished with the floral dance being danced in the streets and in and out of the pubs and finished on the Old Castle Green. This was followed by ballroom dancing in the Guildhall.

In that same year, Mother's cousin, Aunt Bessie to us, who had emigrated to Australia with her in 1913, offered to teach me the piano. As she lived nearby, this would have been quite possible. However, Father's reaction was negative, saying "What does he want to do that for? He will never stick at it." The cost was his main worry, but Aunt Bessie, I think, was prepared to teach me for nothing or sixpence a week. I have wished many times since then that I had been given the opportunity to learn to play the piano and to read music.

After school we were only allowed out to play until 6.00 p.m. in the wintertime or earlier, and we had to be in by 7.00 p.m.. During the summer, it was 7.30 p.m. and when we got to the age of nine years, it might be 8.00 p.m. unless we were at choir practice on Mondays and Fridays. If we were not in by a specified time, our parents came looking for us and we were smacked if we were late and sent to bed without a drink or anything to eat.

Some of the street games I remember were "Jack, Jack Show a Light", "White Horse Kick" and "King", for which we used a ball. We also played football and cricket and at times made up our own games, some of which were handed down from generation to generation because, in the early 1930s, there was no such thing as radio or television.

Another event once a month was the silent films on a Saturday morning in the British Legion Club, close to St. Mary's School. We saw such famous films as Charlie Chaplin and later, when sound was added, cowboy films with Hop-A-Long Cassidy and Roy Rodgers. I think we had to pay threepence in those days. In later years, if there was a decent variety show at the Palace Theatre in Plymouth, Mother and Father would take us by bus into the city where we were treated to tea in Goodbody's Cafe in George Street, before going on to the theatre. We saw quite a number of entertainers who had been on the radio variety shows, but their material was not quite the same as Mother had heard on the radio and she was disgusted by their innuendo or suggestive jokes.

Each year we always paid several visits to my Aunt Ada and Uncle Claude, who lived in Tavistock. On one such visit, we did not get home until about 8.30 p.m. having been away since early morning. Father came up later in the day after closing the shop at 1.00 p.m. for his half day. He went out after our return home and went first to the Police Station where he was a Special Constable.

He was greeted by the Station Sergeant with "Your boys have been at it again and this time they are in real trouble." When Father enquired "What have they done this time?", he was told that we were responsible for throwing stones at the grammar school building at the end of Castle Green and breaking some windows earlier in the day. Father replied, "Well, they must have a good throwing arm because, since early this morning, they have spent the day in Tavistock and have only just arrived home." It turned out that another family of boys and girls had done the damage and blamed us for it. We could only assume that it was the Aldridge family children we went to school with and sometimes played with. That family consisted of three sons and three daughters.

One of the daughters was called Elsie, who was a month younger than me, and one day, we got into an argument about the stone throwing and in consequence, I picked up her new china doll from her pram and smashed it on the ground. In later years, during the War we worked together in the N.A.A.F.I. and she told about the doll incident to other members of the staff. We were both in the same class at school along with Phyllis Taylor, who also worked with us in the N.A.A.F.I..

There was another time when Father found out that Ron had been smoking, so, to set an example to us other three not to do the same, Ron was made to sit by the fireside and smoke five Woodbine cigarettes, one after the other, while the rest of us sat and watched him. Whether he smoked them all I do not remember, but Ron was very sick and ill after that experience and he did not touch another cigarette for many years.

This did not deter the rest of us from trying ourselves to experiment with smoking. What we failed to realise was that clothing was very easily impregnated with smoke which, to a non-smoker, was soon detected. Awkward questions were asked by Mother. We denied it, of course, but you could not fool Mother; she smelt the smoke in our clothes.

As my brothers got older and had their own bicycles, they very often cycled to Bigbury-on-Sea or Bovisands to go swimming in the summer months. Sometimes they cycled to Cadover Bridge on the moors to bathe in the river there and occasionally camped overnight. As I could not ride a cycle then, nor did I have one, I was left at home, which at times was boring not to have anyone to play with. There were times also when my brothers would not let me go out with them, saying I was too young. In fact, they did not want me to get hurt because of my leg, as they were going on a very long walk or climbing trees, that's what they told me.

Even to this day, I have always hated the cold, dark winter time, so, from the middle of January, I am glad to see the evenings start drawing out to herald the springtime. That has always been my favourite time of the year to watch the spring flowers all coming into a blaze of colour to brighten up the gardens and countryside to free us from the cold, dull, dark winter nights.

Every year, in late February or early March, we had the annual spring flower show in the Guildhall and one year I won a prize for my hyacinth bulb planted the previous late-September. This was followed by an evening concert when two men played the spoons and bones, and the school children entertained with songs and recitations.

The next event to look forward to was Shrove Tuesday pancakes, then Good Friday, for two reasons. When we were old enough, we could get up very early, about 5.00 a.m., and go to the main street called Ridgeway, to see the crowds that had come walking, roller skating and cycling from Plymouth to get hot-cross-buns from Griffiths Ye Olde Bunne Shoppe, made from a secret recipe. There were street singers and dancers, also Morris dancers and all kinds of impromptu street theatre to entertain us, as well as brother Ron with his pea shooter. This went well until about 9.30 a.m., when we had to go and get ready to be in church for morning service at 10.00 a.m..

Another treat for me was Mrs. Phasey's delicious hot-cross-buns. She was the caretaker of the Guildhall and a customer of Father's, and I had to fetch the buns just out of the oven.

After lunch we set off as a family, my parents, brothers and I to the fields to pick primroses to decorate the church for the next day, Easter Saturday, in readiness for Easter Day. Each year we tried to pick more bunches than the previous year; but we did average twenty-four bunches a year. When we reached the field it was a glorious sight to see all the hedges covered in masses of primroses, a sea of bright yellow with speckles of green leaves and grass. Yet, after we had finished picking, the hedges still looked untouched because we left the smaller flowers to grow.

We tied the bunches onto a long stick cut from the hedge and carried some in a basket. In the copse adjacent to the field we would pull bunches of bluebells. They were pulled, not picked so as not to damage the bulb (learnt from Mother). Our flowers were always put in one of the windows on the north side of the church next to the profile in marble of Sir Joshua Reynolds.

At Rogationtide, in May, we always went to the parish boundaries where a choir boy would be bumped and the parish council would beat the bounds with long bean poles. Prayers would be said and hymns would be sung. It was Wally who would be carrying the gold cross at these events.

In the summer months, as we got older and had more freedom from home, a group of boys (about twelve of us in all, if not more) used to go camping in a field on Saturday afternoons. The first thing we did was to go to a shop and buy eggs, bread, bacon, lard, tomatoes and a box of matches. We then set off for the field and made a camp fire and cooked all this food in a frying pan. It was agreed that we all took something along for the camp. We never brought any food from Father's shop as some of the boys thought he was a grumpy old man.

Anyway, my brothers and I would have been banned from going if he had known what we were going to do. The farmer came in the field on one occasion and told us to put the fire out and get out of his field, which we did. As he knew most of us, he told our respective parents. However, when Father was told that we had been in this field with the other boys, for once his reaction was to say "Boys will be boys and I will have a word with them."

Two other characters I recall were a Mr. and Mrs. Elliot, who lived in Dark Street Lane. They were both small in stature, no more than five feet tall, and each walked with a limp. Our nickname for them was "Danky" because of their height. He limped on his left leg and she on her right leg, so he was always on her left side when they were out walking together and it was comical to see them. If they had changed sides, they would have kept bumping into each other and possibly hit their heads together.

I was about ten years old when my aunt and uncle sent me my first invitation to go to Newton Abbot to stay with them for a weekend during half term in October. I spent many holidays there with my cousins, Peter and Sheila, after this and it was a new-found freedom from Father, which I made good use of. Sometimes, Peter and I would get up before 6.00 a.m. and walk across the park to the station to watch all the steam trains. They were magnificent feats of engineering and seemed so powerful when going full steam to Plymouth in the west or north to Exeter. Peter would come to Plympton and stay with us during August, usually for a week, and this also let me off the hook from Father.

Prior to that, we did not know what going on holiday was, other than seaside outings with the Sunday School, the choir, and the Oddfellows, which were always looked forward to in the summer. The Sunday School always alternated with Paignton one year then Teignmouth the next, and on arrival back in Plympton, we always had a pennyworth of chips from the chip shop on our way home from the railway station.

Aunt Enid and cousins Peter and Sheila always travelled down from Newton Abbot and joined us for the day. On one visit to Teignmouth, Mother lost my brother Frank. He went off on his own after lunch and we could not see him anywhere. Bruce and Frank Lowden were sent off to look for him, but they came back without him. While all this was going on, I was playing on the beach with Ida and Barbara Lowden. Mrs. Lowden and Mother got worried but hoped that Frank would turn up eventually. Sure enough, when we got to the station, there he was waiting for us. Mother gave him a real ticking off, and I don't think he ever did it again.

The choir outings, on the other hand, went further afield to places such as Looe, Par Sands, or Bude, in Cornwall. In other years, we would go to Exeter, Exmouth or Brixham, but always we had to attend a short service of thanks before being let loose in the town or on the beaches.

One year, when I must have been eight or nine years old, the Oddfellows took us by charabanc to Wembury beaches for a day trip. This charabanc had a canvas roof and was open at the sides so that, when it rained, the roof leaked and the rain came in by the sides as well. Sons from other families came with us and altogether there were about ten of us, and we kept together all day on the beach. Because of my leg, I was not allowed to paddle in the sea, so when the other boys and my brothers decided to go for a swim and scramble over the rocks, they left me on my own to look after their clothes, with instructions that I could have *one* cigarette for doing so while they were gone. Some of them had clubbed together to buy the cigarettes and matches. On their return two hours later (it seemed much longer to me), they found that I was being very sick, having smoked three or four cigarettes and I had used up the box of matches (beaches are windy places). There was a lovely large spread of a picnic tea for us at 5.00 p.m., but I was too ill to look at it. I think I just had a cup of tea. I was not feeling too bad when we got back home and nothing more was said and we did not tell our parents.

A week later Father went to get the weekly order from another shop that he supplied in Fore Street whose son had been with us to Wembury. Imagine his surprise when he was asked if I was feeling better. Someone had let the cat out of the bag about my being ill the previous week, and it was my eldest brother, Ron, who got a roasting from Father for not looking after me properly. I also got told off for smoking and sent to bed again. Father must have had a fixation about sending us to bed for doing wrong. You see, being a close-knit community, as the parish was, you could not keep a secret for very long.

The next year, the Oddfellows decided on a trip up the River Tamar, sailing from Millbay Docks in Plymouth to visit Calstock. This was the riverside hamlet with old iron mine workings (Mother decided to come with us and help with the teas). In the 19th Century, the iron-ore was mined and sent from there on barges down the River to the Docks in Plymouth. I assume for export.

The other summer highlights would be hay-making time in June, making piles of hay and jumping into them or making a large circle and playing games around it. Then in the summer holidays in August, we would go picking blackberries for jam-making and blackberry and apple pasties.

When I went out to play in the summer evenings I would call on my school friend Roy and we would ride his four wheel trolley down a hill to see how fast we could go. At other times, we played with spinning tops, or skipping with other school friends, a mixed bunch of boys and girls; or we might go looking for wild animals such as rabbits in the fields.

On the Saturdays in the summer the Grammar School Old Boys' cricket team played cricket on the School field down a narrow lane from Long Cause around the corner from the shop. Father supplied the food for the afternoon teas for the two teams and we had to carry the food to the pavilion in a large wicker basket. On one such Saturday I went along with Ron, then we were walking around the boundary watching the game when someone called out, "Look out!" Too late, I was hit on the head by the cricket ball. Ron took me home where a cold compress was put on the bruise.

On the 21st September each year, the Patronal Festival of St. Maurice was celebrated in church. That was when I used to cycle out into the countryside with Frank and pick mushrooms very early in the morning. One year we were so early that we sat in the hedge and watched the mushrooms emerge from the ground while we each had a cigarette. When we got home we weighed them on the scales in the shop and we had about 12lbs. Father thought he would sell them in the shop, Frank and I said "No". Mother sided with us, agreeing that they were not for the shop but were for our breakfasts, and the remainder we had promised to sell to some of our friends. He was very upset because he knew the three of us were against him. When Mother had cooked those mushrooms they were deliciously full of flavour. We then had to go to church for the morning service.

In October, we would have the Harvest Festival. The gifts of fruit and vegetables along with the specially-made harvest loaf were always given to the children's wards in the hospitals in Plymouth. Father, I must admit, had a flair for decorating a basket to hold the fruit in, and each year it took pride of place on the table in the centre aisle in church for the children's service in the afternoon. He never made two alike.

Many years later at harvest time, I went to the Salvation

Army Hall for their festival service with my school friend, Roy, and his mother and older sister. When that was over I was invited to stand out in front and help with the auction of produce, mainly I think because they thought I had an idea of what prices to go for, by virtue of working in the shop. I told Mother where I had been but nothing was said to Father. In the shop next morning a lady came in and told Father what a good job I had done at the auction the previous night. He thought it was wrong for me to have gone because I was a member of the Church of England and not of the Salvation Army.

During the autumn we would gather horse chestnuts to play conkers with, and that was followed by gathering eating chestnuts. We would sometimes get a few that had white skins which we kept in our trouser pockets so that they would turn a brown chestnut colour.

November saw the Guy Fawkes celebration on the 5th and was usually celebrated with a few fireworks let off in the street until about 7.00 p.m.. Then it was indoors for a hot drink before going to bed.

About the middle of November, excitement and anticipation began to build up for Christmas. Father decorated the shop window with all kinds of gifts and decorations for Christmas which had been delivered in good time. (He had a flair for this.) The centre piece was an eighteen inches tall Father Christmas whose head nodded back and forth when the clock mechanism was wound up. There were displays of fruits such as apples, oranges, clementines, and boxes of dates, a barrel of grapes packed in fine cork, all kinds of nuts, boxes of chocolates, toys, and games like Snakes and Ladders, Ludo and dominoes.

During this time we were all on our best behaviour so as not to miss out on the great day. About a week before Christmas we helped to put the decorations up in our sitting room. Some of the decorations we made ourselves either at home or at school. On Christmas Eve we watched Mother preparing the cockerel and Christmas pudding, mince pies, and most of the vegetables ready for cooking the next morning. Then my aunt and uncle would arrive with my two cousins from Tavistock to stay for the next two or three days. Later, our other Aunt, Susie (Mother's youngest sister), would arrive.

We only had three double beds in two bedrooms, so Mother, her two sisters (Aunts Ada and Susie) and my cousin Winifred slept in one bed, in one bedroom, and somehow the rest of us shared the other two beds, two men and five boys!

Father also ran a Christmas draw each year, so after the shop closed on Christmas Eve, we would have our dining table full of all the prizes, some of which were those that had not been sold in the shop. About six to eight customers would stand around the table and each one took out a ticket for each prize and this would take about an hour or so.

Christmas morning arrived and it started by seeing what our stockings held, usually an orange, an apple, a few nuts, sweets and chocolates. We did not have a tree, and in the early years, the presents came wrapped in brown paper. One typical year I can remember I had a book, hair brush and comb, and a tank wind-up toy. That was from my aunts and uncles and Mother (note nothing from Father, his contribution being the filled stocking and the food, i.e. the 7-8lb cockerel, and the rest of the food from the shop).

We all went to the 11.00 a.m. Sung Eucharist in church, leaving Mother with the cooking. Some of us had already been to the communion at 7.00 a.m., Mother included.

Any silver three-penny pieces found in the pudding were collected and sent to the B.B.C. for the Wireless for the Blind Christmas Appeal. We usually sent ten shillings. Bruce has still got forty-eight silver three-penny pieces that Mother saved from the puddings. (Ten shilling note sent to the B.B.C. was the cost of one licence). After tea, we had games around the fireside, such as conundrums, spelling bee, and pulling crackers then reading out the jokes etc..

Boxing Day was more relaxed, with a walk around the country lanes after a cold dinner with mince pies. Then it was home for tea and more Christmas cake and mince pies with clotted cream.

Every New Year's Eve the church bells rang out the old and rang in the New Year. Because we lived right by the church, it was the one night that Father relented and let us stay up late. He knew that we could not get any sleep until the bells had stopped ringing, usually about 12.30 a.m..

We then had Christmas parties to look forward to. First, it was the day school on the last day of term; then the Sunday School held in the church room. The games were all the same at either party, Pass the Parcel, Spin the Plate and Musical Chairs. Postman's Knock came in later years. After that came the choir party, about fourteen boys, including the probationers, let loose in the choir master's house, a good tea and a slide show. Last but not least, came the Oddfellows' party where we had a magician and the same party games. We were always sent home with a large stick of rock and a jaffa orange, plus any prizes that we may have won.

From the summer of 1936 we were all expected to help in making the ice cream in the mixer which had a set of blades in the container. This was turned by a wheel on the outside of the mixer which was packed solid with ice. As the milk began to thicken into ice cream, it began to get harder to turn the wheel. Although we were only small boys when we began this, we were called weaklings by Father if we complained. Our reward might be an ice cream but that depended on the mood he was in.

In his store, Father had set a gin trap and caught a rat; it was caught by its hind quarters. When he went to kill it, he hit it several times over the head with the coal shovel and I shall never forget the squealing that it made. It was so bad that I ran indoors to get away from the noise.

At the age of eight, my brother Frank one lunchtime ran from the junior school playground into the road, was knocked down by a lorry and became caught in between the double back wheels. Luckily for him he was double-jointed so he did not have any bones broken, but he was badly cut, a stomach muscle was ruptured and he received a cut to the back of his head. Mother and Father were fraught with worry and my other two brothers and I were looked after by my Mother's cousin, Bessie, while they went by bus to the hospital in Plymouth to visit Frank. He stayed in hospital for about a month before he was fit enough to come home and, after another two weeks, he went back to school.

It was about this time that Father made us all members of the Oddfellows Friendly Society. We had to have a medical, this was to enable Father to get us all individually insured with an insurance company for seven years.

In December 1936, I was admitted to full membership of the choir in time for Christmas.

When I was seven I was deemed old enough to begin helping my brothers to deliver groceries on a Saturday morning to those customers who had placed their orders earlier in the week at the shop. Father had made a two-wheel trolley for this and he insisted that he knew best how to load it. Once we were on our way and out of sight of him and the shop, we rearranged the load our way. The customers paid us for the order. The bill heads had a red emblem at the top advertising Jacob's biscuits followed by Father's name and the name of the shop.

It was during that same year that I set fire to the old skittle alley floor boards at the rear of the shop whilst my parents were away for a day. I had managed to get hold of some matches and empty potato sacks and set them alight. My eldest brother, Ron, was looking after the shop and me at the time, but somehow I went missing until the smoke from the fire frightened me. Ron smelt the smoke and guessed where I was. Buckets of water soon dowsed the fire and no real damage had been done. I think I got a hiding for the trouble I caused, I know I was sent to bed without any tea.

A year later we four brothers were responsible for setting light to the toy cupboard, and Mother put it out with a saucepan of water. Both parents were very angry about this and we all felt the weight of their hands, as well as a verbal telling off.

The toy cupboard had a very strange, distinctive musty smell in it and it made you feel ill if you stayed there too long. If I was to think of that cupboard now, the smell would return.

As I got older and my brothers were either swotting, doing homework or games on Saturday mornings, it fell to me to haul the trolley around Plympton, full of groceries. When I could, I got Wally to help me and we met quite some distance from the shop, so that Father would not know that I had help. Strangers and people who knew me, and noticed the iron on my leg and saw me struggling, would take pity on me; but although I felt embarrassed, I had to ignore them and still had to do it. We only had tips, if any, from customers as a reward. We dared not tell Father about the tips, so we spent the money on our way delivering the groceries.

I know I have not said very much about Mother during all these years. Father being the dominant one, she kept a low profile most of the time. She kept the house clean and cooked for us, or took us to Plymouth about once a year for new clothes when needed. I have seen Mother beg Father for money to get us new clothes. His attitude was to pass the clothes down to the next son and just buy clothes for the eldest one. Mother once replied, "Well dear, if you want your sons to go to school in rags, that's entirely up to you. I refuse to do any more mending or repairs for them." Whereupon Father would grudgingly give her enough money for new clothes plus bus fare (seven pence return for Mother and four pence return for each of us).

Mother was always there should you need any advice or to nurse us when we had chicken pox or measles. I once had acidosis, which meant that everything I ate turned into acid in my stomach. I was put on a diet of poached eggs, bread without the crust or butter most days, until I was gradually weaned back onto a normal diet.

August 1937 saw the departure from home of my eldest brother, Ron. He left Plymouth on the overnight train to Liverpool to join his first ship, the "Clan MacPhee". Before the train left, he gave me sixpence and told me to buy Bruce, Frank and myself a two-penny ice cream tub each from Father's shop.

Ron was to become a cadet deck officer with the "Clan" Line Shipping Co. and make himself a career at sea. He was sixteen at the time and it would be three months before we saw him again, by which time he had been to South Africa and back to Liverpool. Whenever he wrote home he told us of the countries and towns he had visited. I used to look up the map of the world to find out where these places were. I believe because of my interest, it stood me in good stead at school with my geography.

Ron did not want to join the Merchant Navy, but because he had seen an article about the Trinity Pilots, Father assumed that was what Ron wanted to do, so he signed him up for the Merchant Navy. During his apprenticeship, Ron pleaded many times not to carry on, but Father was adamant that he should stay in it; he hated being in the Service.

Chapter Five

1938

Soon after Easter I went into hospital for the second operation on my foot. While I was there, the liner "Queen Mary" anchored overnight in Plymouth Sound. We were able to see it from the ward balcony and we watched it leave the next day.

This was also the year that saw a great deal of political activity by Germany making demands for various pieces of land lost in the Great War. In early spring, we heard on the wireless that Neville Chamberlain, the Prime Minister, had returned from seeing Hitler in Germany with a signed agreement between our two countries. He made history by waving this agreement to the crowds from the upper window of No. 10 Downing Street in London, saying, "Peace in our time." We saw this on the cinema screen newsreel the following week. It turned out that the agreement was not worth the paper it was written on, because we were at war with Germany within the next eighteen months.

From then on the Government began to mobilise the armed forces in case there was a war and, in general, the armed forces were being deployed all over the country. All those men aged eighteen years or more began to be called up to join the Navy, Army or the Air Force.

From a small child I was never to lose the true meaning of the eleventh hour of the eleventh day of the eleventh month to remember those who gave the supreme sacrifice during 1914/18. We had assemblies at school on that day where we were expected to stand to attention, heads bowed, for the two minutes' silence. So it was of great concern to our country and empire to avoid another conflict if at all possible.

Even amongst these turbulent events, some things remained the same for us childern. In the autumn of 1938 on my way home from school with my brother Frank, we decided to look for horse chestnuts at a tree we knew in the Path Fields. Frank decided to climb the tree and in doing so he went out on a limb which gave way under his weight, and limb and Frank crashed to the ground. Afterwards he soon picked himself up none the worse for his fall.

As you can see, this period in our lives as children was centred around the church, the school and the parish. In the coming year this was all going to change our lives drastically in the country for ever.

Plympton and its residents would never be the same again.

Chapter Six

THE EARLY WAR YEARS
1939-1942

1939 dawned, still with a threat of war. There was still a lot of activity in Europe in the political field with all the governments of the day trying to avoid another conflict, except Germany, which was being very awkward, and occupied countries in Eastern Europe and the Balkans. The League of Nations were having constant meetings in Geneva. As a boy, nearly twelve years old, that did not mean very much to me at that time.

In the evenings we went to see the adults learning how to put out incendiary bombs with the aid of a stirrup pump. This was carried out in a garage at the rear of the police station and these people were called fire fighters, who had all volunteered for this task.

Life carried on as usual with the school activities, and Bible Class on Sundays, between the church services, which I attended, having been in the choir by now for just over two years. We also had our annual seaside trips with the Sunday School, choir outing and the Oddfellows.

My visits to hospital were still every three months after my second operation on my foot the previous year, losing another two months from school.

There was a great feeling of apprehension and expectancy all the time that it would not be long before we were at war again. Everyone was hoping that Germany would not bring Europe into another conflict, but it all felt too ominous.

In late-August, Mother took me on a visit to Tavistock for a few days to stay with Aunt Ada, while my two brothers, Bruce and Frank, went camping at Cadover Bridge with some friends, leaving Father on his own working in the shop.

While I was in Tavistock (it being right on the moors), I was able to go on my own for walks across the moor. There were also times when Mother and Aunt Ada came with me. At other times, I would walk into Tavistock, which took me about fifteen to twenty minutes, and have a look in the shops with Mother or go into the park and walk by the River Tavy. I returned home with her at the end of August and on the 1st of September, Germany invaded Poland.

Germany was given an ultimatum by our government that if they had not withdrawn their troops from Poland by 11.00 a.m. our time on 3rd September, we would then consider that a state of war would exist between our country and Germany. There was no withdrawal by Germany and Mr. Chamberlain broadcast the news to the nation from 10 Downing Street at about 11.15 a.m.. We were, from then on, at war again against Germany within twenty years since the First World War had ended.

At the time of the declaration I was in church for the Sung Eucharist with my brothers, Bruce and Frank, and my friend, Wally, so we were not aware of the news until the Rector gave an announcement before the sermon, saying a prayer for peace. When we got home just after 12.00 noon, Mother and Father had heard the Prime Minister speak for about five minutes. Other bulletins were made at hourly intervals. That afternoon, after lunch, I went to Bible Class carrying my gas mask; I was the only one to do so.

Soon after the outbreak of war we were issued with Identity Cards (I still have mine) and food ration books soon followed. One of the first casualties of that war was a Plympton man called Arthur Glyddon, whom my parents knew as at one time he was a member of the St. Maurice Men's Club.

We had many false alarms of air raids when the siren went off during the first few months of the war, but it was good practice in a way for later years. When we were in school and the sirens went off, we literally had to drop what we were doing and make a quick and orderly evacuation to the shelters until the 'all clear' was sounded. This disrupted lessons a great deal, to the annoyance of the teaching staff. The siren was fitted to the roof of the police station in Ridgeway so we could see it as well as hear it from the school.

In September, the aircraft carrier "HMS Courageous" was sunk in the North Atlantic by a German U boat submarine, being our first major loss of the war at sea. The ship was a Devonport-manned one and I went to school with some children whose fathers were serving on that ship but did not come back. That was my first real baptism of the war.

Going to school we saw many reserve soldiers who had been called up, getting ready to go to France to defend the Franco/German border. We did not know at that time they were headed for France, all we knew was that they were going away to fight in the war.

We began to be avid listeners to the B.B.C. News Bulletins on the wireless so that we knew how the war was progressing. Until the end of 1939 we used to hear reports like 'All quiet on the Western Front'. We gave many sighs of relief when hearing that. Christmas came but there was not the usual enthusiasm to celebrate. We just went through the motions of celebrating with the Christmas dinner and having some relations to stay for two or three days. The attitude in the community became a little blasé and we were hoping that the war would soon be over. Little did we know then that it was to last for almost six years.

1940 began without celebration and the church bells were now silent. They were only to be rung if we were invaded, to warn us of enemy invasion and occupation by the Nazi forces. The Government introduced Double Summer Time so, at the height of summer, it was still light until nearly midnight. The idea was to give farmers more time to gather their crops and to deter the Germans with their air raids on us at night. When the evenings began to get lighter, I began to learn to ride a bicycle with only a front brake, and my friend Roy persuaded me to ride it down a hill. I called out, "How do I stop if I feel I'm going too fast?" Roy answered, "Jump off the pedals and put your feet on the ground." I could only put my left foot down and I burnt a hole in the sole of my boot and nearly twisted my foot in the process.

Both Roy and I were interested in two girls in our class at school who both came to school by 'bus from Brixton. This was a village between Plympton and Yealmpton about four miles from Plympton. The two girls were friends; one was very thin and the other was rather plump. One day at school we said we would cycle out to Brixton to see them in the evening. They never thought we would because they believed that we were joking. However, we did cycle out to where they lived and surprised them. We soon realised that they were not interested in us so we said "Cheerio" and cycled on from there through Yealmpton and back to Plympton.

Besides this, my friend Wally and I were friendly with two girls who attended the church services on Sundays, and we would meet them after lunch on the Castle Green and go for walks together. Their names were Pat Palfreeman and Christine Jane.

Christine was a Sunday School teacher and was the youngest of us. She also went to a private school and this year she was given a bicycle for her birthday. One day after School she set off to cycle home when she collided with a school bus and as a result, died from her injuries. She was only twelve years old. This had a profound effect on the three of us. At her funeral service, I was in the choir and Wally was the server. We had been given special permission from school to attend the service.

During this same year, my school master, Mr. Brown, hauled me out in front of the class very roughly as being one of the class causing a disturbance. I was told off and caned. My reaction was to say, "That's right, Sir, pick on the weakest one in the class," whereupon he went red in the face and told me to go and sit down. He left the classroom to compose himself I suspect, but some of the class said that I did the right thing to stand up to him. Unknown to me, Mr. Brown was a Special Constable like Father and he related to him that evening what had happened that morning, admitting to Father that I had made him look small in front of the class. Father's reaction, when he got home, was to give me a hiding and I was told never to answer back to a teacher again. I was not allowed to explain my side of the story. The real culprits got away with it.

I thought of being obstinate the next morning and refusing to sit down in class because of the hiding I had had, but I decided not to. From then on, I took a dislike to Mr. Brown and I was careful not to upset him again, and I was not picked on as much. Mr. Brown was our music teacher as well as form teacher and he knew I was in the church choir so he used to make me get up and sing solos during most of the music lessons. I was nervous to begin with but I soon got used to it and to a certain extent, I enjoyed singing on my own.

Like my brother, Frank, before me, I had to learn a descant to a hymn with five other choir boys. This we had to sing at assembly and the teaching staff were impressed by the result. It stood me in good stead for later years in learning tunes other than the melody.

When I was due for another check-up at the hospital, for once Father said that I could go on my own because he had a very important meeting that he could not miss (I learnt later that it was a Masonic Lodge meeting). I was delighted, of course, to go on my own but I was only told by the consultant, "Come back in three months." On leaving the hospital, I hastened to the 'bus stop to get home as soon as I could to avoid being caught in a possible air raid, which could happen at any time.

Plymouth and Devonport had begun to get air raids occasionally and some of the bombs would stray around the countryside near us. On our way to school the next day after an air raid, we would look out for shrapnel from the shells fired by the heavy ack-ack gun which we called Big Bertha, stationed on top of a nearby hill called Dorsmouth Rock, about half a mile away.

In April, Mr. Chamberlain resigned as Prime Minister and Mr. Winston Churchill was asked to form a new Government. He did so by setting up a coalition cabinet until the end of the hostilities.

In this year also we had a contingent of Indian soldiers camped just outside Plympton at Chaddlewood, complete with their horses. They brought them through the parish streets on their way to the country lanes to take them for exercise. They only stayed a few months before they were sent to another region of England or to the Middle East.

We then had the trauma of the Dunkirk evacuation of the B.E.F. and other allied soldiers after the collapse of the fighting in France. We in Devon were not too affected by this other than seeing some of the survivors arriving back from France, but we did see the newsreel of it in the cinema, if it was open, or photos in the newspapers.

While all this was going on the German U boats were sinking the allied shipping in the Atlantic, between England and America, which made shortages inevitable. In all, we lost 50% of allied shipping throughout the War in the North Atlantic. We tried to carry on as normal but we began to notice the shortages of food and raw materials, especially from abroad.

It was shortly after this, with the threat of an imminent invasion, that the Food Office designated Father's shop to serve the Parish of St. Maurice with food rations. He was given extra stock on non-perishable food, such as sugar and tinned food, in case of that eventuality. All the other shops in the Parish would be closed until further notice.

It was at this time that certain foods began to be unobtainable and were classed as scarce and they were put under the counter, if we were lucky enough to get any (tinned fruit was one item). Many is the time that white lies were told because of this situation, so that they could be kept for the registered customers only.

Air raids then began to get more frequent at night so sleep was not possible until the 'all clear' sounded.

'Dig for victory' became a motto and at school, we all had to help in setting up a vegetable plot. It was a very large one, almost the size of a football pitch, and we did some of the preparation during the weekend. From then on, gardening became one lesson that was done by rotation, in which each class took part, so gardening was done every day. We kept chickens at the school and when the hutch was cleaned out, the manure was placed into a large empty dustbin with a tap fixed at the bottom. We covered the contents with water and left it to stand for a month or more. This liquid manure was then watered down and fed to the vegetables and my, did we get good results! I had never seen onions so large in all my life before and the potatoes and other root crops such as carrots and swede did very well, as did the runner beans, cabbages, cauliflowers and leeks, which were all used in the school canteen. That was real organic gardening which, at that time, we did not recognise as such. Also available were other fertilisers, such as horse, cow and pig manures from the local farms. It was termed by one school master as putting back into the ground that which you had taken out.

At home, Father turned part of the old skittle alley into a vegetable garden and the produce was well fed with cow manure from a local farmer's herd of cattle. They were customers of Father so it was a case of 'help thy neighbour'; we got dairy produce in return.

By September, the Battle of Britain was being fought over the skies of the Home Counties, Kent and London.

We were still having air raids at that time but as we approached the winter, they began to abate, mainly because of the bad weather. Christmas that year was not celebrated as in pre-War days. It was a very austere affair but we did manage to have a bird on Christmas Day, thanks to a customer who kept chickens. Father was promised one because he gave her the vegetable waste from the shop.

By this time, Father won the franchise to have a Sub-Post Office on his shop premises. Its official name was Plympton Erle Sub-Post Office, Plympton Erle being the original name for Plympton.

1941 arrived and I was full of apprehension and expectations, not knowing what lay ahead.

This was the year that I had been waiting so long for, to, at last, be old enough to leave school; but I would not be able to leave until the end of July.

Before that happened, Plymouth had a visit from the King and Queen in April on a Thursday. That night from about 11.00 p.m., the Blitz really started over Plymouth. It went on relentlessly all night long, the Germans thinking the King and

Queen would still be in or near Plymouth. However, they had left long before the raid started. The next night we had another long raid that lasted several hours.

The next morning (Saturday), I went with Bruce and Frank to Plymouth because we could not believe the stories at school that we had heard about the damage done to Plymouth, nor could our parents believe the rumours they were hearing. Very little news about the raids was mentioned on the national news.

We could only get so far into the city by bus and we had to walk the rest of the way to get to the city centre. The devastation that met our eyes in the city centre was unbelievable - all the streets that we knew were strewn with rubble and obliterated, and most of the shops that we had known were burnt out shells of their former selves; other buildings which were still standing were cordoned off. All the gas, water and electricity supplies were either cut off or reduced in power.

The oil depot at Oreston on the coast was hit and it burned for days afterwards. This helped the German bombers immensely to get to the targets of Plymouth and Devonport at night. Mother had to cook on an open fire, with a cast-iron saucepan (there being no gas), and boil all the water before we could drink it. This went on for weeks until the services were restored.

The citizens of Plymouth began to leave the city by their thousands and some ended up in our schools as evacuees, where they were given food and shelter. Others pressed on further into the countryside or on to the moors to get food and perhaps shelter.

At first we could not go to school, so we went along to help feed the evacuees and make them as comfortable as we could. Then a compromise was worked out with the Grammar School Governors and our Senior School Governors. The Grammar School pupils were to use the school buildings in the mornings and we were to use the school in the afternoons, from 1.30 to 4.00 p.m..

The blitz continued throughout the summer and, if we did not have a raid, it was because it was the turn of Exeter, Bristol, Portsmouth or Southampton to be blitzed.

In early evening the buses left Plymouth for the safety of the countryside. Many came to Plympton and parked in the lanes. Because we lived by the bus terminus we knew many bus crews and our parents invited them in for a cup of tea and whatever food could be found in the shop, we helped to make sandwiches for them. Sometimes there were as many as twenty or more in our sitting room, which was cramped to say the least. However, they all slept on the buses until the next morning. Prior to this many buses were lost in the air raids.

One night, when a raid was on, I was at the George Hotel with the landlord's son and another school friend, both of whom were called Roy, we were in the same class at school together. We were in the kitchen playing snooker on a small table when my brother Bruce and his friend Frank Lowden called at the Hotel (they were air raid messengers) to take the two of us home and said "Did we know there was a raid on?" "Yes", we said, but we thought we were all right because it was Plymouth that was being bombed and not Plympton. We could hear the shrapnel falling around us as we went down the hill towards home. On our way to school the next morning we looked for the shrapnel but never found any. At school, after each air raid, someone always managed to find shrapnel and bring it for us to see. We collected incendiary bomb fins as well.

On another night raid the German bombers tried to lay mines in Plymouth Sound, but many aircraft missed their target and most of them landed in and around Plymouth and Plympton, which made the blast do all kinds of queer things, bouncing from wall to wall in a zigzag fashion. Several that did land did not go off and one landed in a field opposite my cousin Winifred's house. She and her daughter, Julie, were evacuated like all the occupants in the houses nearby, so we had Winifred and Julie and the dog with us until the mine had been dealt with. The ground was very soft at that time, due to recent heavy rain for several days, which could be the reason why some of the mines did not explode on impact.

Torquay and Paignton and the surrounding countryside had what became known as 'hit-and-run' raids. The planes dropped their bombs and went back to France in a matter of half-an-hour or less. Coming home from school one day, when there had been a few days lull from air raids, we heard this droning noise in the sky and when we looked up, it was literally covered with German aircraft heading west across the Channel towards France, out of range from our ack-ack guns. We tried to count them and after we got to about two hundred, we gave up. I shall never forget that sight; I don't think I have ever seen as many aeroplanes at the same time in the sky since then.

That evening, on the news, we heard that Bristol had suffered a severe daylight raid by several hundred aircraft.

Plymouth was the most bombed city in the country outside of London and morale got to a very low ebb. It was decided that Mr. Churchill would visit the city and see the damage for himself. This lifted our spirits up to some extent, but we still had many more raids to suffer from for quite some time after his visit.

This was also the year that Frank and I, being old choir boys, heard about the Youth Choral Club who gave concerts to the elderly and the general public and raised money for the war effort. We both joined and when Bruce was on leave from the Royal Navy, we got him to come along as well. We met every Tuesday night in a classroom at the Grammar School and we averaged about sixty members to start with. About twenty were young men, some of whom, like us, had sung in church choirs. We had a marvellous time in that choral club travelling around South Devon giving concerts in schools, churches and village halls, and a mental hospital. Many of us (myself included) chatted the girls up hoping to get a date, but possibly because of the War, some were reluctant to get involved, but we all remained good friends.

Our repertoire was very varied, ranging from Christmas carols and hymns and other religious works, excerpts from Gilbert and Sullivan operettas, student songs, Handel's "Messiah" and "Silent Worship", to national songs including works by Elgar such as his "Pomp and Circumstance" numbers One and Four. "Jerusalem" was another favourite as were "The Fishermen of England" and "Juanita".

As you can see, over the years, this broadened my knowledge of music a great deal, having to learn many songs and ballads etc. that were new to me. Later, when my voice broke, I had to learn to sing mostly bass. Since then, I have always enjoyed listening to two-and four-part singing and, of course, singing rounds. Listening to any music today, I am always listening for the harmony and picking out the various instruments and not the melody. Choral music is still a great favourite of mine as is church organ music My brother Frank had a good tenor voice and he sang solos such as "Bless this House", "Young Tom o' Devon" and "Glorious Devon".

After each rehearsal I had to walk home sometimes on my own in the blackout and I was not too good at it. I seemed always to bump into lamp posts or a Belisha Beacon, or trip over the kerbs. At other times I managed to get most of the way home with other members of the choir.

Mr. Wellington was the musical director, a school teacher in Plymouth by day. He picked two other lads and myself one season to learn a descant which we had to sing and be heard with and above the rest of the choir. Quite a tall order, but, with rehearsals at his house with supper laid on, we soon learned the descant and we could be heard very well.

At the final rehearsals in the hall sometimes he would give the choir a piece to sing and go to the back of the hall and call out, "I can't hear the words." We had no amplification to help us in those days and it sounded much better without such aids. Mr. Wellington firmly believed that the words were just as important as the music and he emphasised this at every concert warm-up.

Mr. Wellington had a brother who had a very deep, rich bass voice and in some concerts, they would entertain us with comic duets, "The Two Gendarmes" being one of them.

When we had given a concert in Plymouth, on our way home on top of the double decker bus, we would sing impromptu songs not in our proper repertoire, such as "One Man Went to Mow", "Green Grow the Rushes Oh", or "Now is the Hour", which some of us harmonised while the girls sang the melody. Other passengers would applaud our rendering which, in a way, was a good advert for the choir.

During this time Bruce and Frank bought records of the Americans Glen Miller, Bing Crosby and the Tommy Dorsey

Band. They also bought many other popular English bands and vocalists, but not Vera Lynn. Contrary to popular belief, she was not well liked by the civilians, who preferred Petula Clark; at least we did. I did not start my collection of records until much later. We played these records on a gramophone in our bedroom which was over the shop and sometimes the customers would remark that we were in good voice if we had been singing, which was often.

In August, I did leave school but what to do to get a job? That was the big question. Father found out that a local chemist and Parish Councillor was looking for an errand boy for four hours a day, two in the morning and two in the afternoon. That was the first of several jobs that Father thought he ought to have a hand in where I was concerned. This being my first job in the outside world, my wages were seven shillings and sixpence a week, and the rest of the hours each day I had to help Father in his shop at NO extra pay. I was told to give Mother five shillings a week towards my keep and keep the rest as pocket money. I was too young to argue with this, but Mother did not always take money from me for my keep and that was our secret. At the chemist, if there were no medicines to deliver, I was given the task of thoroughly washing out the empty medicine bottles, a thankless job that I detested, there being no hot water. Eventually, I left there in November.

I managed to get a job as a temporary postman for the Christmas rush which ended after the Christmas morning delivery. I called in to see my cousin Winifred and her husband, Joe, and I had a glass of port wine with them. I then had to get home in time to be on server's duty at the 11.00 a.m. service. Early in the New Year I went to work full-time for Father.

On 7th December, Pearl Harbour in the South Pacific was attacked early in the morning by Japanese war planes; this brought America into the War. America also declared war on the Axis powers in Europe.

Chapter Seven

A TURNING POINT

When I started work in Father's shop in 1942 one customer who came in happened to be the Rev Cyril Armitage, and during a conversation between my father and him it transpired that he was the brother of Noel Gay. Noel Gay was the composer and lyricist of "Me and My Girl" in the 1930's, which included such songs as "The Lambeth Walk" and "Love Makes The World Go Round". He was a chaplain in the Royal Navy for the duration of the war. Prior to the war he had been the King's chaplain and precentor of St Paul's Cathedral.

I worked in the shop from just before I was fifteen years old. As soon as I started work in the shop, he began arguing with me. This went on for months and Mother was the peace maker between us, sometimes telling Father not to hit me, which he had threatened to do. All throughout the year, we were still having air raids, sometimes only short in duration and much longer ones at other times.

What with the Blitz and working under duress with Father, I realised that we would not get on together in the shop, so later in the year saw me getting a job as an apprenticed gents hairdresser. Father had a hand in me getting that job, too, and he told my new employer, Mr. Matthews, not to pay me more than fifteen shillings a week. Mr. Matthews replied, "Bert, I'll pay him what I think he is worth and not what you suggest." At the end of my first week, Father could not wait for me to come home and his first question was how much had I been paid? When I replied, "£1 less insurance stamp," he said that I was being over-paid. He only paid me twelve shillings and sixpence, and yes, half had to go to Mother. Was it any wonder the embarrassment I felt when I could not pay my way when I was out with my friends at dances. I could not afford to buy raffle tickets or a drink, the dances being in aid of the war effort. Sometimes these dances ended in a brawl between soldiers, sailors and airmen, who were the worse for drink. Some were from the Allied nations, French, Polish, Norwegian, Dutch, and later on, black and white Americans.

During that year I stuck it out at the hairdresser's but what everyone did not realise when I started there was that most of the hairdresser's equipment, clippers and other tools like scissors, were right-handed and I am left-handed.

I celebrated my sixteenth birthday there and on that day, I was given a very large brown, paper parcel. It took me ages to unravel the amount of paper, only to find a small tobacco tin, inside of which was another piece of paper with five Woodbine cigarettes inside. After that I decided to light a cigarette. As I did so, a policeman who was having his hair cut asked me if I was old enough to smoke. This was all a joke played on me by the other two staff in the shop and the policeman. The atmosphere there was more relaxed with a lot of leg-pulling going on most days.

At the end of that year I left on good terms with Mr. Matthews, who realised that because I was left-handed, it was very awkward for me to carry on. I then went to work at the 'Coy Pool' in Marsh Mills alongside American soldiers. They were a great bunch to work for and the American doctor who gave me a medical was so fascinated by the condition of my leg that he asked other doctors to examine it. I was kept well supplied with American cigarettes and chewing gum during my brief stay there. I did not pass the medical because they considered I could only do light duties, so I regretfully had to leave.

It was in the autumn, in late October, that the Battle of El Alamein in Egypt had been won against the German and Italian Forces. Mr. Churchill announced that the churches could ring a peal of bells in celebration of what he termed "The beginning of the end."

To start the year of 1943 I was out of work, luckily not for too long. Without Father knowing at first, I applied to join the N.A.A.F.I. not long after my seventeenth birthday and because of my shop experience, I was accepted. Father was surprised that I had got the job without his help.

By this time Bruce had been in the Royal Navy for two or more years, but Frank had failed his medical for the forces, so he was sent to Bristol to work in a munitions factory. I, for my part, was posted to the N.A.A.F.I. canteen on H.M.S. Drake in Devonport Barracks. The one thing that has stuck in my memory of my time there was having lunch most days of mashed potato seasoned heavily with pepper, on top of which was a large gammon steak, which I thoroughly enjoyed. About two months later, I was given a long weekend leave and told to report to Beechwood Camp N.A.A.F.I. canteen manager at 0800 hours on the Monday. This was a shore-based camp on the edge of the moor, set in a wood close to the village of Sparkwell, and it was just three miles from home.

Two girls on the staff there were in the same class as me at school so we could reminisce about the school staff and other boys and girls that we knew, and if they had joined up in any of the forces.

Imagine my surprise when I learnt that the manager, Bill Phillips, was a Freemason like Father; but unlike Father, Bill treated me with respect and we got on very well together almost to the point of being pals.

I settled into the routine very well for the rest of that year and for my first Christmas, there was rather an amusing event, if you could call it that.

We had three young men from the Acton area of London on the staff who, we had assumed, joined the N.A.A.F.I. service to avoid enlisting in the services. On this particular festive season, they decided to decorate their billet with Christmas decorations that they had managed to get hold of. On their afternoon off they had done this and then invited the staff on duty in the galley to see what they had done. So, Elsie, Phyllis, Nancy and I went to their billet to see what the decorations looked like. We did not venture inside but looked at their efforts from the doorway.

It took us a little while to notice that in amongst the decorations were blown up French letters (condoms) which they had got from the sick bay. As soon as the girls spotted the condoms they screamed and ran back to the galley as fast as they could. They could see the funny side of it and laughed it off, but it made them more cautious as far as those Acton lads were concerned.

There were few times that all four of us were at home together, and on this occasion Ron had just arrived back from Gibralter. We were in our bedroom while they unpacked their gear and out came a box with a set of ladies' yellow silk underwear. This was a very scarce item to get hold of during the war, but encouraged by us, Ron tried on the bra' and slip. We burst out laughing seeing him in this get up, which brought Mother up to the bedroom to know what all the laughing was about.

She was at first very embarrassed to see such a sight, but soon saw the funny side of it and asked who was to be the lucky girl friend to get such a gift. Ron was non-committal. During 1944, one of my jobs twice a week was to take the money to the bank in Plympton by the civilian lorry, then go into Plymouth and Devonport to the breweries and load up the lorry with the beer. We always had a free pint of beer at the brewery while this was being done by the men who worked there. One week, the lorry driver, who was known as 'Bungy Friendship (he was a Norfolk man), got me drunk on three pints of mild by lunchtime. What Bungy did not know was that I had had no breakfast that morning, having got up too late for it. He was a heavy drinker and on our return to camp, I was put to bed to sleep it off until it was time for me to go home at 5.00 p.m.. Bungy could hold his beer all right, but that particular day I reckon he would have been banned from driving had a drink/drive ban been in force in those wartime days. He had drunk more than the three pints it took to get me drunk.

Bill Phillips, the canteen manager, was frustrated not knowing whether I had been to the bank until the next day. He greeted me with, "Are you feeling better and what about the £100 for the bank?" I replied that I went to the bank first before going to the brewery, and gave him the banking book with the receipt.

Mother found out that I had been drunk and, to say the least, was very annoyed with me, but as far as I know, she never told Father.

Beer in those days was kept in wooden barrels and I learnt how to tap a barrel and most aspects of bar work. We had two bars, one for Chief Petty Officers and Petty Officers, the other bar for Ratings and Able Seamen. Other than that, the work was very similar to working in a shop.

Bill had to go into The Royal Naval Hospital in Devonport for an operation for varicose veins and he phoned me one day from the Hospital and asked me how the stock of 'Nutty' rations was in the canteen. 'Nutty' was the naval slang word for chocolate. I took stock of what we had and the temporary manager asked me why I was taking stock. So I explained what I was doing and he was not too pleased about it. The following week, when I went for the beer I went with 'Bungy' as usual and I had two boxes of chocolates with me. I went into the Hospital in Devonport and saw Bill, who told me that he was selling the 'Nutty' bars to the patients, which increased the canteen sales. This in turn increased the amount we could stock the canteen with.

On another occasion, when Bill was back in charge, Father asked Bill at a Masonic Lodge meeting if he could spare him some cigarettes to sell in the shop. Bill asked me to take them to Father. This I did at risk to myself in taking them out of the camp. I had one hundred Player and a hundred Senior Service cigarettes. They cost Father 1/6 per packet of twenty, which he sold at 2/4 per packet in his shop. He, in effect, was making a pound profit. All I got from Father was "Thank you", and I was livid. He did not understand that I could have been dismissed from the service for taking such a risk bringing out such stock. So I did the next best thing, I took forty cigarettes for myself from his stock and refused to give him any more. I made the excuse that a sailor was caught at the camp gate trying to take out more than his ration of cigarettes.

Because I had 'native' leave each day, meaning that I went home every night at 5.00 p.m., I had to help in the galley every afternoon. The cook was a Cornish lady who was called Nancy. She was a very portly person with a happy outlook on life and we always got on well together. It was her job as cook in charge of the galley to make and cook buns and cakes etc. to be sold in the canteen. I learned from her how to make rock buns to a wartime recipe and other recipes. The rock buns lived up to their name. One day, after cooking them, we were caught playing football in the coal yard with the unsold buns. Mostly, if they were not sold they were broken up and soaked in water overnight. The next day mixed spices were added and the mixture made into 'Nelson' squares on a two foot square baking tray, lined with pastry and covered with a pastry lid.

Sometimes I would stay at the camp overnight so that I could go to the dance in the village hall in Sparkwell, which had a pub next-door. The other members of staff and I would have a drink in the canteen, then walk to the village pub about five minutes from the camp and have a few more drinks. The pubs in wartime closed at 10.00 p.m., so it was on to the dance next-door until 11.30 p.m.. On some occasions we would go back to the manager's office after the dance and have another drink and talk until early next morning.

One chap told us about his experiences in Africa serving in a ship but was glad to be back in England. Later on, I would go home more often and go to the George Hotel with Bruce if he was home on 'native' leave stationed in the barracks, and have a drink. N.A.A.F.I. pay then was £1/10 shillings a week less stoppages; beer was 11d or 1 shilling a pint; spirits were 2/3d a nip, if you could get it. Twenty cigarettes would cost 1/9d for 'Woodbines', 'Stars' and other brands such as 'Players' and 'Senior Service' cost 2/4d a packet of twenty.

Quite a number of the canteen staff lived on the camp because they came from all over the country including three from London. These three lads thought by watering the beer and keeping the profits, they could get away with it. What they failed to realise was that they put far too much water in the barrel and made the beer very watery. I had witnessed them doing this in the morning and did not say anything.

That evening, the three London lads were on duty on the

.en's bar and the seamen complained to the manager, who
.ted the beer and knew straightaway that the beer was not
.aleable. He immediately told the culprits that they would be
sacked forthwith and sent them off duty. He managed the bar
himself then for the rest of the evening. The next day, I had to
take the lads to Devonport to the N.A.A.F.I. H.Q. to get them
discharged. If they passed a medical, they would be called up
into the army.

One weekend that I shall never forget was when we had all
been out on a 'bender'. I don't recall Bruce being there but
Frank was because most of those with us were at school in the
same class as he was. We finished up in the Air Raid Wardens'
Post (the pre-war men's club) on the Old Castle Green about
midnight Saturday and some of the R.A.F. boys with us
produced a bottle of port and a bottle of sherry. Between us we
drank the lot and we staggered our separate ways home about
3.00 a.m., knowing that we would all be back at camps and
airfields by 23.59 hours on Sunday. Frank went back to Bristol.

The next Wednesday, there was a one thousand bomber air
raid on Cologne and Dresden in Germany and other cities and
all the R.A.F. chaps that we had been with the previous weekend
took part in that raid; most of them *never* came back. We did
not know about this until a week or so later when the casualty
lists had been published. This makes you feel more involved
with the war and much closer to it when this occurs.

Of course, this was also the year that the Second Front opened
on 'D' Day, 6th June. Quite a number of men in the forces from
Plympton were either injured or lost then and later on, as they
advanced across France and the Netherlands. I watched the
Typhoon fighters fly over Plympton in formation on their way
out to shoot up the railways in France in support of the ground
forces. I counted them out and I counted them back again and
because there was virtually no resistance from the German air
force, they usually all came back. The airfield was at Yelverton
on Dartmoor, which is about half way between Tavistock and
Princetown.

Quite frankly, I do not like talking or being reminded about
the war years very much, because I think it made me a timid

person. When I hear people talk about the few bombs that they experienced in the war in fairly remote places, they don't know what it really is like to be in a Blitz. To hear some of them talk you would think that they had been in all the air raids throughout the war.

In December I had to have my call-up medical in Plymouth because I was within three months of my eighteenth birthday. I was in uniform and when the doctor asked me, "With a leg like that, what are you doing in uniform?", I replied that I was working in the N.A.A.F.I. in a naval camp classed as a civilian and I was allowed to wear the uniform to enable me to enter the camp where I was stationed. I was classed as Grade Four, which meant that I was unfit for active service in the armed forces; no square bashing for me. It is also the reason why I was turned down for service overseas to the Middle East that I volunteered for. I had heard that canteen staff were needed in Egypt at the time.

During the rest of 1944, everywhere in Europe, the Allies were advancing on all fronts of the war zones slowly but surely from the east and the west. The Allies in the west had a setback when the battle for Arnhem failed with a great loss of life and prisoners were taken by the Germans. Undaunted by this setback, progress was being made elsewhere in France, Germany and the Netherlands, and the Germans were in retreat, leaving small pockets of resistance in some towns and cities. In Eastern Europe, the Russians also were advancing on all fronts, liberating towns, cities and, above all, countries. The Italians by now had surrendered to the Allied Forces.

By Christmas time, permission had been granted by the Government that the church bells would be rung when all hostilities had ceased. Christmas itself in England was celebrated for the first time in six years almost like pre-war, knowing that the war could be over perhaps in 1945. As if by magic, we began to see more of the usual food connected with Christmas time appearing, such as mince pies and Christmas puddings, cakes, sausage rolls and, of course, a chicken.

We certainly made up for what we had missed all through the war. I think Mother was very good at hoarding scarce luxuries in food and she got so used to it that it was hard not to stop later as food began to get more plentiful as time went by.

* * * *

At the start of 1945 we could sense that the war in Europe at least would end that year. We had to wait until May before the war in Europe ended and May the 8th was declared a Victory in Europe Day, a national holiday, after the signing of the unconditional surrender of the German forces on Lünenburg Heath two days before.

I went on duty at the camp canteen as usual that morning but by 10.00 a.m., Ron and Bruce came and fetched me home as I had been given the rest of the day off. Ron had draped his car in the Merchant Navy flag and we toured around Plympton visiting my cousin and her family and other friends.

That evening I believe we made merry at the street parties and in one or two pubs, but in general we were greatly relieved to know there would be no more threats of air raids over us.

The following weekend I arrived in uniform at my Aunt and Uncle's home in Newton Abbot. I had a 72-hour leave pass. That evening, Saturday, there was to be a V.E. celebration party in Milber Woods with food being cooked on a camp fire. I had a group of girls around me all the time and when the party was over and my cousin Peter asked me what was the attraction, I said, "It's probably the uniform and not me."

Aunt Enid and Uncle Bill were glad to see me but asked me that the next time I went, would I take some rations of food with me. They found it a struggle to make the rationed food last the week, especially with an extra mouth to feed that weekend.

In June, we had a visit from Father's two sisters, Aunts Lil and Anne, and Uncle Frank, Lil's husband. They had been invited to Ron's wedding to Phyllis Griffiths, but Phyllis broke off the relationship two weeks before the wedding.

Each evening Mother and Father entertained my Aunts and Uncle with my brother Frank and myself playing card games etc.. Aunt Lil was a heavy smoker and liked her drink and we were plied with the same by her. Remember, I was now eighteen, but each evening Father would say to me, "Norman, go to bed" or "Norman, Bed!" This got so bad one night that Aunt Lil turned on Father and said, "For goodness sake, Herbert, stop nagging Norman, leave him alone." Then she turned to me and said, "Have a cigarette and fill your glass with another drink." We then carried on playing cards, and Father never said another word to me. I must admit that I enjoyed those evenings.

One night, Father went to a meeting, so Aunts Lil and Anne asked Mother if Father's attitude to me was always the same. Mother replied, "I'm afraid so."

When the atom bombs were dropped on Japan early in August that hastened the end of the War in the Far East. Bruce was serving on H.M.S. Lock-Eck in the Far East at the time, and the ship's Captain took the Surrender of the Dutch East Indies from the Japanese, who signed the Instrument of Surrender on board the main deck, witnessed by the ship's officers and crew.

Here in England we were trying to pick up the pieces and rebuild the bombed cities and towns, but there was a shortage of men and materials. It was going to take a very long time because there were still many thousands of men not demobbed from the forces who could do the work.

The N.A.A.F.I. bosses in Devonport had drafted me to a naval camp at Wembury Point and it meant that I had to 'live in' on the camp. I had to run the whole canteen on my own, which was small compared to Beechwood Camp, but I was still expected to cook the rock buns and Nelson squares. I could only get every other weekend off and I relied on Ron to bring me home in his car. Wembury Camp was very isolated with little or no public transport, and the camp lorry was not always available to take one on shore leave.

After the War in the Far East ended and Bruce had come home, Ron came out to fetch me and Father was with him, so were Bruce and Frank. Talk about a surprise, Father sat between Frank and me in the back seat on the way home. Back seat drivers!! Father would win hands down every time. There was no one worse! Every bend, every junction or corner, Father would tell Ron what to do, "Turn left here or turn right there, slow down, stop." You name it, Father said it. In the end, Ron or Bruce muttered, "I wish he'd shut his bloody mouth." Frank and I grinned and Father said, "What's the joke?" and one of us passed it off as something we had just seen that we had passed. Father must have forgotten that we knew these roads from the Camp very well, Ron and Bruce having cycled along them before the War.

We called in to see our cousins, Winnie and Julie, and found that Winnie's husband, Joe, had returned home from Ceylon.

Not long after that the N.A.A.F.I. wanted me to go to Cornwall to work at another Naval/Air Force base, I think it was Culdrose, but I refused to go and decided to leave the service for pastures new. However, I had not reckoned that Father would once again impose his authority on me. Two men from the N.A.A.F.I. H.Q. in Devonport came to our home to try and persuade me to stay on. Mother understood me better than Father, she knew what I was trying to explain and sided with me. He, on the other hand, became heavy-handed in his manner towards me, but I didn't give in and after the men had gone, I told Father that I knew what would happen and be expected of me once I went to Cornwall. On reflection, could the two men have been Freemasons!!!? I wonder!!

I was still in the choral club and enjoying it to the full, but now the War was over the interest began to wane. Some members had emigrated and others had got married and eventually the choir ceased.

Shortly after this I went to hospital for another check-up and a secretary there suggested that I apply for a training course at St. Loyes College for the Disabled, in Exeter. I did apply and I was accepted for training as an electrical domestic appliance repair trainee on a six months' course.

Chapter Eight

DISCORD, DISILLUSION, DEPARTURE

I left home in February of 1946 and went to Exeter to begin my training. My first impression of the place was, "What am I doing here?" Compared to a lot of the trainees, I considered myself an able-bodied man.

Most of the men were there as a result of injuries sustained in the recent War, legs missing, or an arm lost. One man was riddled with shrapnel and could collapse at any time as it was too dangerous to remove the pieces. Another very cheerful man, Welsh by birth, lost both his legs just before D Day when he was in Italy. Some were the result of coal-mining accidents and some, like me, had polio, very much more severe than mine, or other kinds of paralysis. A few were chair-bound from mental illness. For all their adversities, they were a happy bunch of people to be with and we put on concerts or shows to entertain ourselves at weekends.

On our first morning of training, our tutor emphasised that he could not teach us in six months what took him seven years' apprenticeship to learn, and that he was still learning about new and improved electrical appliances.

I went out on a date with a local girl who worked in our canteen and while we were out, we passed her uncle and aunt, who said goodnight to both of us. On our next date, she said that she had a message for me from her uncle, which was 'Had I found the key to the starboard watch yet?' I asked her how did he know about that? She replied it was he whom I had asked at

Beechwood Camp when I was in the N.A.A.F.I.. He was a carpenter in the Royal Navy. It was a leg pull that I fell for at that time. The result was that I was invited to tea the next Sunday and I went there quite often after that until we parted company for good. I then went out with a girl trainee from Chudleigh, Devon, who was born with only part of one arm, the other arm was perfect. I went home most weekends and I would meet up with Wally, who would fill me in with news of what had happened while I was away.

In June, I managed to get home midweek so that I could attend Ron's wedding the next day. He was to marry Joyce Quick whom he had known for a year or more. He had risen to be a Second Mate by this time in the Merchant Navy.

When it was time for us to leave St. Loyes at the end of six months I had a routine medical which we all had when leaving. It was suggested that I see my surgeon as soon as possible in Plymouth when I returned home. The reason soon became apparent. My leg had grown so well in length that I did not need a 1/ inch cork build up on my boot any more. I was told I could wear shoes for the first time since the age of four, and that I need not wear the iron any more, the night shoe being discarded many years beforehand.

I cannot even now describe how I felt full of joy, and 'elation' comes to mind. No more would I have to drag that heavy boot and iron around with me. I had to wait six weeks for the shoes to be made and it felt like walking on air with the shoes being so much lighter. If I could have afforded it, I expect I would have had a good drink to celebrate.

I soon came back down to earth having no job to go to. St. Loyes College had found me a job in Oxford and yet again, that was thwarted by Father. He refused to let me go and told the College that he could get me a job locally (Freemasons' help again). So back home to Plympton I went and Father had got me a job at thirty-five shillings a week with a plumber, who said that he did electrical repairs as well. From the word go, we did not get on with each other, and when Father met him at his next Freemason's Lodge meeting, he was told that I was no good ('Bloody useless' is what he actually said). Father tackled me about it and I said I did not like being sworn at in front of the people we were working for. I admitted to him that I did something wrong and my employer swore at me, so I walked out of the house and went home. Needless to say, I did not go back again and I had to return the kit of tools that I had been given when I finished in Exeter.

By this time we were well into 1946, and it was agreed by Father and me that I should work for him until I had found another job. Much later, I realised what a bad move this was to be. As the winter progressed and we reached January and February 1947, we saw the worst blizzards in Devon in living memory, the snow being in places up to four feet deep. It was worse on the moors with villages being cut off with no gas, water or electricity. This also disrupted all the road and rail services for many weeks, and I found it difficult to keep myself warm.

Later in the year Bruce and Celia had got married and I had to look after the shop with Mrs. Morris while Mother and Father went to Wheaton Aston for the wedding service. Frank sang a solo of "O Holy Father" to the tune of "Ave Maria", which he had been practising in our church. The Rev. Herbert Ernest Bennett was not too pleased about the adaptation.

The Palace Theatre in Plymouth was not too damaged from the air raids and it soon re-opened to entertain everyone with live shows. When I could afford it (which wasn't often), I went to the Theatre to see various radio stars that I had heard on the radio. I made friends with an ex-Grammar School boy, a little younger than myself, and he would talk about nothing other than emigrating to Australia on the £10 assisted passage, which had been set up by the Australian Government shortly after the War had ended. His enthusiasm rubbed off onto me and I mentioned it at home.

Father's reaction was to mention all the obstacles that I would have to overcome. The following reasons he gave me were: Who would sponsor me in Australia? How would I cope with paying for medical care and treatment when I needed it? and above all, what kind of work would I look for? and would anyone out there risk employing me? Mother tried to put plus ideas forward but to no avail. You can guess from that, that I did not emigrate, I don't think my friend did either.

I had left the choir four years before, but I was still a server alongside Wally in church. We were still doing our evening walks after church of three miles to the Miners Arms, where we would have a drink and eat a hot pasty. They cost 9d each and were worth every penny of it after the walk. I missed Wally a great deal when he was transferred to Bath. We kept in touch by letter, and we still went for our evening walk when he did come home whenever he could for a weekend.

I had become disillusioned with the way Rev. Herbert E. Bennett was conducting his new way of taking the morning Eucharist service. For a start, he wanted to be referred to as 'Father Bennett', which I totally disapproved of because he was not married with a family.

The next thing that he introduced was the use of incense which then made our church a high one. I could never understand why incense was used other than to keep bats from the belfry. I carried on for a while still serving when I had to until I could not stand the smell of the incense any longer as it was making me cough quite a lot. I went to see Rev. Bennett by appointment and told him I was resigning as a server.

He asked me on what grounds had I come to this decision, and I said that I did not agree with the use of incense and calling him 'Father'. He said that he had been using the Anglo-Catholic service for a number of years, but I replied, "I was brought up in the Church of England faith and not the Catholic way of religion." I then left the vestry and I began going to St. Mary's Church in the other parish. This I continued to do until I left home in 1952.

Because of the very bad winter of 1947 the church authorities decided to replace the old coal boiler heating system with gas heaters fixed to the walls, so a fund was set up to raise the money. The Rector announced it from the pulpit at Evensong and said that a donation of £5 had already been given by an anonymous giver. Next morning, in the shop, Father was in the Post Office side talking about the new church heating system to someone who was in church the previous evening. Imagine my surprise when I heard Father proclaim with pride that he was the anonymous giver. Mother was in the kitchen behind the shop, working and she heard what he had said. All she would whisper was "and I had to beg for money from you to clothe the boys before the War started."

I was expected to do most of the work in the shop. The rationing was still on and weighing the various amounts of butter, margarine and lard was a tedious job which I did after the shop closed. The ration coupons were another headache, sorting them out and sending them to the food office. We could not get further supplies until the coupons had been redeemed. Once a week, I had to go to the bacon factory in Plymouth to get about 20lbs of the various cuts of bacon and sometimes I had to wait for the bacon to be sliced. The factory did all their own processing with the bacon and the aroma of smoked bacon made my mouth water. I was not strong enough to carry such a weight to the bus stop, so I took my time carrying the basket with frequent stops. I would miss a bus rather than hurt myself. When I got home I was greeted with, "What took you so long, where have you been? I can do it quicker than that." I explained that the factory was very busy and I had to wait my turn and that I had missed the bus. After one such trip with this greeting, I lost my temper at this and I told Father, "In that case, you can go next week and I'll look after the shop." Mother intervened between us and she was to be the peacemaker from then on.

A little while later, Father found out that another shop owner, Bob Friendship by name, was also a customer of the bacon factory and he offered to take me in his van with him each Monday afternoon. To Mother's and my amazement, Father agreed and each week said to Bob, "Don't keep him out too long, I want him back here." When we left Bob said to me, "If it takes me all afternoon, your Father will have to wait." Bob had customers to whom he had to deliver which meant we got to the factory later than planned, so he made excuses to Father why we had been so long, and as he left he would wink at me. Bob once told me it was unfair of Father to expect me to carry such heavy loads. He, like me, had a disability in his leg or hip, but I never really knew what it was and I would not ask him.

On another occasion, Father was talking to a customer about me and remarked that I had cost him more than the other three sons put together. I said, "That's not my fault. I can't be blamed for having a gammy leg." I got a telling off for that and I told him he should not be discussing me with the customers. He also told the Rector's wife that if it were not for his wife expecting me, they would have returned to Australia in 1926. So I said, "You can't blame me for that." When the shop was empty I was told I didn't have to pass remarks like that in front of the Rector's wife. What else was there for me to say? I felt that I had to stick up for myself.

Our G.P. was a Dr. Owen and he lived across the street from us. He had a daughter called Susan and a son called David. In those days I thought that Susan was an attractive girl. She and David very often would come to buy stamps and postal orders etc. for their father in the Post Office, and I got to know them quite well. Years later, Susan married a Lieutenant Dental Surgeon in the Royal Navy. David went on to medical school, qualified as a doctor and eventually he entered Parliament as an M.P., representing Devonport. He became one of this country's youngest Foreign Secretaries. He is now Lord Owen, elevated to the peerage for political services to the country.

Food continued to be rationed and yet the War had been over for two years. One reason for its continuation was the amount of merchant shipping that was lost during the War. Fresh fruit and vegetables became a lot easier to obtain now that the market gardeners were growing a lot more.

Working in the shop sometimes had its lighter moments and one trick I know is the one I played on Betty Shorten. She had recently had all her teeth out and when she got her new dentures, she came into the shop smiling. So I said, "They look very nice Betty. I expect you feel better now that you have them." I then offered her a very sticky toffee to eat on the way home. She thanked me for the toffee and left the shop to walk home. The next day when she came into the shop, she greeted me with "Norman, you bugger!!!" I said, "Why Betty, what *have* I done?" in all innocence, she then replied, "I began to chew that toffee yesterday and halfway home both my dentures got stuck together and I had a hell of a job to scrape the toffee off my dentures when I got home." I burst out laughing and offered her another one, which she refused in no uncertain language. When Mother and Father heard what had happened, they saw the funny side of it.

Another leg-pull of mine was the upside down penny prank. In damp weather the penny stamp machine would get jammed because of the glue on the stamp sticking to the drum. This happened one day to a girl the same age as me. I told her that she had put the penny in upside down in the machine. After putting the machine right I told her that the penny must face the machine with the King's head and nose facing it in the upright position. I did this myself and the stamp was duly delivered. To my knowledge, that girl, now a woman in her sixties, still believes that I was telling the truth.

At the Constitutional Club in Ridgeway each Christmas a Christmas draw was held with upwards of thirty prizes or more to be won. A list of numbers was put up on the notice board on December 1st, costing sixpence to enter. Father would have a game with the Jack and five other cards face down on the table and each person put sixpence on a card. Whoever had put it on the Jack won 3/- and six entries on the draw. Father won many times so each sheet of numbers had his name on most of them. This particular year he won the first six prizes or more, which included an 18lb turkey and various bottles of wines and spirits. He sold the turkey and some of the other prizes, remarking he did not want the turkey because he had got a cockerel on order for Christmas. When he got home and told Mother what he had won and that he had sold the turkey, she was livid, telling Father that she had never tasted turkey and that he should have brought it home for the family to have. As you can imagine, this spoilt Christmas in more ways than one, especially for Mother and the rest of us. Father was not very popular for quite some time after that.

Chapter Nine

PARTY TIME
& A NEW BABY ARRIVES

1948 was going to be another milestone for me in that, being the youngest son, there was to be a large party to celebrate my twenty-first birthday. In previous years, when my brothers reached twenty-one, we only had a small celebration tea because the War was on and goods and services were very tight. It was decided that my birthday would be a celebration for all four sons. Invitations were sent out to about one hundred people which included, at Frank's and my request, most of the members of the choral club, including Mr. Wellington, the musical director, and his wife and daughter.

Unfortunately, about a month before the big day, Mother had to have a serious operation of which I for one was not told the nature. I had a discussion with Father and my brothers and we agreed to postpone the event until later in the year when Mother would, by then, be fully recovered; also, that Ron could be home for it. When we told Mother what we had decided to do, her immediate reply was, "No, you must have it on Norman's birthday as arranged." She was quite adamant about it.

We went to see Mother in hospital on my birthday, March 3rd, in the afternoon, and I had put on my new double-breasted suit for her to see (I felt like a trussed-up turkey). We then went home to get ready for the party, which was being held in the Guildhall. Mrs. Phasey, the caretaker, was there and the refreshments had been arranged by her. She put on a very good spread with Father's help, with some of the food coming from the shop. A bar had been set up in a side room upstairs, with a nine gallon barrel of beer and bottles of spirits and soft drinks. A band was hired who played from the minstrels' gallery. We started with a mixture of old time and modern dancing, and we were all having a good time.

Unknown to me, Bruce had a surprise which was a three foot long silver-plated key which he presented to me (I still have it). I believe I marched around the hall with it on my shoulder, and then I was asked to make a speech. I recall that I mentioned Mother being in hospital and that she was improving; also, that Ron was still at sea and he was also unable to be there, which was another reason to postpone the party.

The choral club also had a surprise for me. They sang 'Happy Birthday' and '21 Today' to me. It then turned into an impromptu concert of our most popular songs. I was not going to be left out so I joined in as well. Our relations who had not heard the choir before were most impressed because we sang unaccompanied.

I had many presents but I wanted my parents to give me a watch. Father said, "No, you will have a signet ring just like your brothers did when they were twenty-one." I had to choose from five rings, watched by the family, and when I picked out the one that I liked, Father remarked, "Trust you to pick the dearest one." My reply was that I had no idea how much each one cost. I myself would still have preferred a watch.

More drinks came my way during the evening and I did get tipsy. When we got home, I tried the 3-foot key in the shop door lock. Father was not impressed, but Aunt Susie and 'Vester could see the funny side of it.

I had also been given presents from some of the customers, including my godmother, Mrs. Reed. I went to see Mother the following Sunday and told her how the party went and how much she was missed; she was pleased that all went well on the day.

The consequence of my twenty-first birthday party was that several of the choral club members were also twenty-one later in the year and I was invited to most of their parties and Frank was also invited to some of them.

I had become very friendly with a local girl called Joan, who was a student nurse at the Mount Gold Orthopaedic Hospital, and my one mistake when I first dated her was keeping her out late. Unknown to me at first, her father knew my cousin Winifred's husband, Joe, and my godmother knew her mother. So my character was in question; this was soon put right when I met her father. He did not ban me from seeing Joan, provided that I got her home by a certain time. This I did, and I ended up nearly every Saturday at their house for supper after which we listened to the radio.

I spent most of Christmas Day 1947 with Joan's family, after cycling to Mount Gold Hospital to meet her when she had an early finish. It was about two weeks before my twenty-first birthday party and things were still being planned when Joan and I parted. I believe she had met someone else. However, this did not spoil the celebrations.

Things returned to normal after the party, back in the routine work of the shop. Mother went to a convalescent home in Crownhill, Plymouth, for two weeks, much to Father's surprise. He thought that she would come home and carry on as before her operation. Aunt Susie had been cooking our meals for us while Mother was away. She was living in a flat in Plympton at the time, so it was not far for her to come. I think it was only the midday meal that she cooked.

About a dozen of us young lads had been nicknamed "The Bachelor Club" earlier in the year. We were always seen together at dances, social and club events. In the summer months since the War had ended we cycled six miles to Bovisands on the coast most weekends and camped overnight. Because I had to work on Saturdays, it was after closing the shop at 6.00 p.m. before I could meet up with the rest later in the evening.

In the winter we held a Christmas dinner and invited a number of local girls along and we had a good time. Ron Nichols took a shine to one girl in particular, called Sylvia, from the choral club and later he married her.

It was the summer of this year that Frank, Wally, Ken Bowers, Bob Southwood, Ron Nichols and myself went by train to Newquay, Cornwall, for a week's holiday. When we got on the train in Plymouth, we heard the Midland accent of a group of girls in our age group. Young men being what we are, we got talking to them and told them to have their passports ready for the customs at Saltash; also for the exchange of English money for the Cornish currency. When they asked why, we said that Cornish people used pixies for money. Besides that, if it was not for the ferry chains on the Saltash ferry and Brunel's railway bridge, Cornwall would float out into the Atlantic Ocean because Cornwall is divided from Devon and the rest of the country by the River Tamar. Eventually they realised that we were leg pulling. It broke the ice and we did see them again at a dance in Newquay later that week.

We went into the water nearly every day but it was Wally who was the one person to encourage me to learn to swim, but I was only able to float. I was too wary of the sea, it being very strong with undercurrents on that north coast.

We met up with six other girls in our hotel who had come down from London and we played as a mixed team for an inter-hotel game of cricket on the beach. We also paired up for the hotel dances, especially for the last night fancy dress dance at the hotel, when Wally won a prize as a scarecrow. I went as Gandhi and my partner went as my wife. Later, after the dance was over, we tried a seance as a joke, but it was no joke when the glass flew off the table. Since then, none of us ever tried it again.

This was the first real holiday that anyone had had since the end of the War, so we all made the most of it and returned home much refreshed from the break from work.

When we returned home, Ron Nichols was looking forward to a date with Sylvia, which he kept quiet about all the time in Newquay. The next week it was back to the old routine of work and I was not looking forward to it.

I had been learning to dance ballroom dancing at a dancing school in Laira, a suburb of Plymouth, with my other school friend Roy. We cycled every week to the venue for a six week course. We paid sixpence a lesson. Wally and I had learnt to do the Olde-Thyme dances at the Guildhall a year earlier, when his mother and sister were our partners.

The church continued with all the festivals for the rest of the year and I was still a server, being on duty most Sundays.

On November 16th Celia gave birth to Alan, my first nephew, and Frank and I were asked and agreed to be Godfathers. The christening was to be on Boxing Day at Wheaton Aston, Staffordshire, which is about thirteen miles from Wolverhampton.

Prior to this the annual Christmas draw was held at the Conservative Club where, between Father and ourselves, we won quite a number of prizes. One prize I won was a duck which I sold to 'Vester, Aunt Susie's husband.

Frank and I went to Wheaton Aston for Christmas and we stayed with friends of Celia's family. After the christening on Boxing Day we travelled back to Bristol and stayed the night with Frank's girl friend's family. The next day she took us to see the Brabazon aircraft which had eight engines and was reputed to be the largest known aircraft in the world at that time. That evening we returned to Plymouth by the overnight train and got there in time to catch the first bus to Plympton.

* * * *

Bruce was now stationed in Devonport Barracks doing his reserve duty because of the Korean War. We had become friends of Mr. and Mrs. Watkins and their two daughters, Joan and Nesta. Frank had been courting Nesta but Joan was made an honorary member of the Bachelor Club. This was because wherever you saw us, Joan was always there. Some evenings Bruce and I spent at the Watson house on Woodford estate which was three miles from home; we always had to walk home because we had missed the last bus, having had a late supper which ended about midnight.

On May 11th Ron's wife Joyce gave birth to Janet, so now I had a niece as well as my nephew, Alan. Janet was the first girl to be born on our side of the family, so this pleased all of us at the time.

After my holiday of the previous year I was now planning a holiday with Derrick Bloxham, who was a member of the

Bachelor Club and also an old school chum of mine. He had arranged to visit Cheltenham and stay with his aunt for two weeks. As I could only get one week off from Father, Derrick spent the first week on his own, but he had booked two coach seats to London for the week we were together.

We left his aunt's house at about 2.30 a.m. and walked to the coach station. We left at 3.00 a.m. and arrived in London Victoria about 6.00 a.m.. Derrick phoned another much younger aunt of his and we met her on Waterloo Bridge and she took us to see the famous Billingsgate Fish Market, which had already stopped trading. Then we went to Covent Garden where we had breakfast. We were left on our own after that because his aunt had to go to work. We spent the rest of the day visiting Tower Bridge, The Crown Jewels and Beefeaters, Madame Tussauds, and Buckingham Palace. We left again at 6.00 p.m. for Cheltenham and that was my first ever visit to London, not knowing then that, in a few short years, I would be living on its doorstep, so to speak.

I was still employed by Father but now he was also thinking of having a holiday with Mother and Aunt Ada and going to London for two weeks. He phoned the theatres in London and booked seats for most evenings. He had to employ a Post Office trained person to look after the post office while he was away.

This was the second time I met Mrs. Betty Morris, who lived in Laira, a district of Plymouth. She and I got on well together, so much so that she helped me in the shop when I was busy and if there was no one in the post office side to be served. Father had to pay her the correct salary according to the Post Office pay scale, which was more than he paid me, which was £2 per week.

When they were in London, Father would phone up and he would want to know if everything was all right. Mrs. Morris and I arranged that she would answer the phone when he rang, saying I was busy in the shop. She was good at convincing him that there was nothing to worry about.

Mrs. Morris very often came out to help after that first fortnight's holiday. I boldly asked for two weeks' holiday, now that he had had two weeks himself when he returned, but I could only have just the one week.

On one of our discussions, I asked Father what had happened to the insurance money on each of us as it matured, particularly mine. He replied that he bought the set of kitchen chairs with my money. When I pointed out to him that the policy was in my name, he replied, "But it was my money that paid for it." I then told him that he took the money on false pretenses, but he could not see that side of the argument.

Mother had in her possession two cameo brooches that were left to her by her late mother, and one day, without telling anyone, Father posted the brooches to Christies, the London auctioneers, for valuation with the possibility of selling them. Christies phoned Father and told him they were worth about £70 each. He was quite pleased about this and told Mother. Mother exploded and said, "You did what!!! You had no right to take what belongs to me without my permission. Phone Christies and get them sent back to me at once, and don't you ever do that again." With that, she went to her bedroom and cried for a very long time. I had never seen Mother so upset before, except for the time about the Christmas turkey, but that was nothing compared to this.

Since my brother Ron went to sea in 1937, we four boys were seldom ever at home together, but there were times when we were and we always made the most of it. Father had encouraged us to join the local Constitutional Club in Ridgeway, and one night we four got to the Club before him to play a foursome at snooker. Ron and Frank were partners, so Bruce and I were the other pair. We ordered drinks at the bar from the steward and we said, "Father will pay when he comes in." We were busy playing and heard Father come into the bar. He ordered his usual shandy and was told he had to pay 4/6. "How much?" exclaimed Father. The steward then said, "Your four sons have had a drink on you, they are in the snooker room." He came in and said in a doleful voice, "I suppose you think that's funny." He liked pulling other people's legs, but he did not like it done to him.

On a previous occasion, one of his friends took out Father's cigarettes from his pocket in the bar and offered them around and finished up offering one to Father. He had only two left from a full packet. He was not amused and had to hide his true feelings.

Father and I were still not getting on together at times. Mother and I tried to persuade him to close the shop at 1.00 p.m. so that he could eat his dinner without interruption. The postman collected at 1.30 p.m. from the post office, so no, he would not close the shop. It was then suggested that he close for thirty minutes, but he was still adamant and would not budge. I refused to leave my lunch and serve a customer one day and said that I did not want to end up with ulcers like him, and if he didn't close the shop, he could answer the bell himself. This caused him to lose his temper and I said, "The sooner I get away from here, the better."

Mother tried a compromise, in that I would have my dinner first while Father stayed in the shop, then we would change places. No, he wanted his dinner at 1.00 p.m. and no later, so we suggested that he had his meal first. It worked for a while but he became more and more dissatisfied, and in the end, it was back to what it was before, interrupted meals.

I kept a check to see how many customers came in and what they spent during the lunch hour, and Mother and I were right - some days he took less than 3/- and no one came into the post office. It took him another three years before he relented and that was after I had left home. He employed a young local girl, as it happened, Barbara Lowden, whose family and ours had been friends for many years.

The one embarrassing thing he did to me was when at any time I said I was going to the bathroom, he always replied, "Don't be long," and irrespective of how long I was, he would call out to me, "Hurry up, Mrs. So and So is waiting to be served." Many times I asked him why he could not serve the customer himself, he was only reading the morning paper. Mother posed the same question, "Why do you embarrass him?" This happened almost daily and in the end, after I'd left home, it had an adverse effect on me. I quite thought all employers would treat me in the same way. Thank goodness it wasn't so! But it made me very nervous as and when I went, expecting to be cautioned on each visit.

During the later part of the year the man responsible for putting up the flag on the Castle ruin flagpole gave up, owing to ill health. At the next parish council meeting it was decided that another man was needed to do this job. Without consulting me, Father put my name forward and said that I would do it for nothing (the fee was £1 per annum). The council were under the impression that I had agreed this with Father. Imagine my surprise on the one hand, Father had said that I would do it, and on the other hand, when a councillor stopped me in the street and said, "How good of you to waive the £1 fee", I replied, "What fee?" It was then I was told that the council paid for someone to put the flag up in all kinds of weather. Of course, Mother did not agree at the way Father had gone about this business and told him so. The result was that I did get paid, and Father must have felt a bit sheepish by his actions from the look he gave me.

I continued to work in the shop but the atmosphere at times was very bad. On the one hand, Father was not too well some days, and for my part, when he was well, I became obstinate and frustrated because my suggestions or ideas to help him for his benefit were not acceptable to him. He did, however, let me have one week's holiday.

As Celia was expecting her second baby in April, it was arranged for Alan to stay with us from the end of February; he was then fifteen months old. He liked being in the shop with me, but one day, Mother caught him mixing the loose soda with the loose sugar under the counter. He quite thought that he was helping me and looked very cheeky when he was found out. Mother was amused by this but it meant we had to watch Alan more closely.

On April 13th Stephen was born, so that meant that Alan would soon be returning to Watford once Celia was well enough.

In July, I went to Newton Abbot to stay with Aunt Enid and Uncle Bill, taking my bicycle with me on the train. Peter was working for the local council and Sheila was still at school and wanted to take up nursing when she left. While I was there, I cycled to Teignmouth via Kingsteignton to see Aunt Susie who had recently had a stroke. Vester was not pleased that I called in. Then I cycled back via Shaldon, where, for a time, the road kept close to the River Teign. I cycled to Bovey Tracey to see my cousin June and arranged to spend her half-day off from work with her in Torquay. We met in Newton Abbot and went by bus to Torquay where we walked along the quay to watch the local men fishing. I was surprised at the shoals of mackerel that were swimming by the quay wall.

I returned to Plympton on the Saturday afternoon, arriving home in time for tea. I refused to answer the shop door bell when it rang, telling Father that I was still on holiday, when he had asked me to answer it.

That evening, I went out to see my friends and Ron Nichols said, "Congratulations Bert (my nickname), I see that you are now in business with your Father." I was flabbergasted and said, "What are you talking about? I'm not in business with him, I only work there." Then it was pointed out to me from the path on the Castle ruin, the sign above the shop window which read, "H. DUNKLEY & SON", which could be seen from where we stood. I went straight home and saw the new sign and asked Father what it meant and why had I not been told by him, but had to find out from outside the family. He replied, "That new sign only meant that you could sign business cheques in my absence when I am away at Masonic functions and council meetings." He had been elected to the Plympton Rural District Council earlier in the year. I disagreed with this arrangement and I told him that he should have discussed it with me first. On Monday morning I had to go to the bank and give a specimen of my signature for the bank's records.

When I told Wally, Ron and my other friends the next evening, they could not believe the way that Father had arranged this in my absence. Ron Nichols, who by now was a qualified plumber, had just had a business agreement drawn up by a solicitor to be in business with his father, with profit sharing and a minimum wage and holidays plus bonuses.

Not long after this, when I was thinking about the shop and post office and I knew Father would be out all evening, I talked it over with Mother what I would like to do. She thought it was sensible what my ideas were and how it would help Father. I thought it over for a few more days and waited to pick the right moment to talk to him. He came home late one night after Mother had gone to bed. I then put my ideas forward to him about the shop. Firstly, he had not been well, ulcers again, and I said he and Mother were not getting any younger. I would do away with selling the vegetables, my reason being too much waste and little or no profit, and replace that with greetings cards for all occasions, more profit and little or no waste. I would want him to keep out of the shop and not to interfere unless I asked for advice, and that he was to be a sleeping partner with a salary. I would give myself one year to make the shop pay its way and if I failed, I would pack up and hand the business back to him and leave home.

Talk about a bombshell. First of all, he was surprised that I could think in such terms. Then he said, "Who put you up to it? Was it one of your friends?" I replied, "No, but I have talked to Mother about it." He then said what he would want me to do with the business and these were his terms. I would have to pay rent for the shop, pay all the rate bills, such as the gas and electricity, and the rent to the landlord (him) and to include the local council rates. I knew that if I had to pay all that, at the present turnover, approximately £100 per week, I would soon have the business in debt. I then proposed putting my idea to his accountant and if he agreed with me, it was to be drawn up legally by a solicitor. This Father would not accept at any price, so I said, "In that case, I no longer have any interest in the shop and when it suits me, I shall leave home."

We sat up until 2.00 a.m. the next morning discussing these ideas, but I realised that I had wasted my time. Deep down, I felt that he would refuse, but I had to try out my ideas on him. Next morning, I could hear he was arguing with Mother his side about what we had talked about the night before and Mother, at one stage, said, "Well, Norman was only trying to help and besides, we are getting older and you won't always be well enough to work in the shop."

After this I told him what Ron Nichols had done about their plumbing business, which his father had done with his grandfather before, so why could he not do the same with me. "Oh no," he said, "out of the question." He could only see his side of the discussion. During this year, Father, on occasions, did not feel very well and at first we thought that he was putting it on; but after seeing his G.P., he was referred to a specialist in Plymouth.

When he eventually saw the specialist, Father must have mentioned that he was a Freemason. On his return home, Mother asked him how he had got on and he said that he was going to the Royal Masonic Hospital in London to get his condition sorted out. As I recall, in pre-war days, when it was suggested that I was sent there, his reaction then was to say that he did not join for charity. Now, the boot was on the other foot and he could not get there quickly enough for himself. In 1938 it was different for me and it still rankles when I think of it and what might have been in my case.

He travelled by train to Paddington in the last week of 1950 after Christmas and went to the Hospital where they found that his blood pressure was high and that for a few days, he had to rest and he only had x-rays taken.

Bruce, who was now living in Watford with his wife Celia and their two sons, after leaving the Royal Navy, went to visit him as did Father's sister, Aunt Anne, who lived in Hounslow, not far from the Hospital.

He had an operation to remove a tumour in the intestine, hence the nausea and not being able to keep his food down. The operation was successful and he went to stay with Bruce and Celia in Watford before returning home to Plympton.

While he was with Bruce and Celia, he was surprised to see Bruce working in the kitchen at weekends, preparing the Sunday lunch. He never understood that Bruce was a good cook, no doubt he learned some of these skills when serving in the Royal Navy. Because of the Korean War and Bruce being on the reserve list for five years, he was called up and he had to report to Devonport Barracks.

Father came home later in early February and was boasting that he could now eat anything, which he could, so no more diet recipes for him and he could eat normal meals once again. This was an enormous relief to Mother, not having to keep him on a diet.

Shortly after his return, he was explaining to Bruce and me what the surgeons had done to him and how long the scar was. Bruce whispered to me, "Look out, he will unbutton his trousers in a minute and show us the scar." He had hardly finished saying it when Father did exactly that. The scar was from above his navel and almost reached his groin. He boasted that that was his thirty-third operation in his lifetime. How true that was we never knew, Mother seemed to think he exaggerated about this.

As Bruce was now on 'native' leave once again, we slipped back to our old war routine of going out for a drink together of an evening, but now we had something to live for, so we did not do any heavy drinking. Frank joined us sometimes if he was not busy with girl friends or playing snooker.

Chapter Ten

I LEAVE HOME

Over the past year or so we had been getting about six to eight of us together and hiring a car on a Saturday evening to go to dances in Tavistock, Ivybridge, Shaugh Prior, or anywhere where there was a dance within a radius of eighteen to twenty miles. Frank Lowden, our driver, used to get his boss to let him have the Austin Ten for this. Frank was a motor mechanic and he kept the car immaculately clean. If the car should break down, we knew that he would be able to repair it, however, we never did break down on any trip. We shared the cost of the car between us and we normally got back to Plympton any time from 1.00 a.m. onwards. Wally would say to me on the way back that he was on duty at 7.00 a.m. the next morning in church to serve at holy communion. Some weekends it was me that was on duty. When I was, I always took Mother and Father a cup of tea in bed before leaving for the service.

When on February 6th, the King's death was announced, I had the flag flying at half mast within minutes. About an hour later Mr. Cyril Crews, the Chairman of the Parish Council, came into the shop and complained about the flag not flying right. I said that it was a very windy day and it was lucky that the flag was flying at all at half mast and "if you can do better, do so." Father for once backed me up. Mr. Crews was not amused and left the shop in a huff.

About a month had passed when we were all at home, it was suggested that we went to the Palace Theatre because there was a good variety show on. Someone around the table asked who was going to pay for the trip and Father said, "Norman will pay," and I replied, "What, on the money you pay me?" A few minutes went by when Father got up from the table, left the room and went to the shop. Shortly afterwards, he called out for me to go and see him. I went to the shop and found him in the post office side. I asked him what did he want me for and he gave me a lecture on what he called my bad remarks about money earlier at teatime and how I did not pull my weight in the shop, getting up late each morning. I said, "Pay me more and I'll get up earlier." Then he pointed to two half crowns on the counter and said, "There is five shillings rise for you. You can take it or you can get out, lock, stock and barrel." I replied that I would take the money for now but I would leave home as soon as it suited me. I then left the shop. Mother asked me what Father had wanted me for and had said to me. I told her about his ultimatum and she went very red in the face. She immediately went into the shop and told him that he should not have spoken to me in those terms. Of course, Ron, Bruce, Frank and Joyce wanted to know what all the fuss was about. Again, I repeated what Father had said and that I'd told him that I was going to leave home anyway. Joyce wanted to know what I was going to do, and all I would say was that I would get myself to hospital for an operation on my foot and take it from there. We did go to the Theatre but I think Father paid only for Mother, himself and me.

Not long after that disagreement, while Bruce was with us, he and I talked a great deal about what action I should take about Father and the shop. I had kept him informed how Father was treating me and also keeping me in a strict regime as regards working in the shop. Bruce was prepared to give me a start in life by letting me stay with him until I could find other accommodation, but he would have to discuss it first with Celia. Whatever Bruce and Celia said to each other, I did not know, but they agreed to take me in until I had found myself a job and then I would have to look for digs elsewhere. This was kept under wraps for the time being until I decided to make my move. Bruce's reserve duty had ended and he left the Navy and returned to Watford to continue his Civil Service position in Customs and Excise, working in London.

I kept in touch with him by letter and Father asked me why Bruce was writing to me. I said that it was between Bruce and myself, but that he would find out one day. I had kept Mother, Ron and Joyce informed of Bruce's letters and when I would make a move, and I soon realised that they were on my side. I was now in a position to put my plan into action. It was time for my half-yearly visit to see the surgeon early in 1952 and I mentioned the problem about my fourth toe which had twisted under the third toe (I made sure that Father was aware that I was having trouble with my foot).

It was a week before Easter when I went into hospital to have the tip of my toe amputated, so Father was without my help. When he and Mother came into hospital to see me on the Sunday afternoon, he asked me how long was I going to be in hospital. I said that I did not know and why was he asking me. "I want to know when you are coming back to the shop," he said and I replied, "I am not coming back." He then asked me what I was going to do. I said that I was going to live with Bruce and Celia and look for work in Watford after they had had their holiday in July. His next question was, "Who is going to keep you until then?" I said that I would live at home until I had heard from Bruce. Father then said, "You will have to pay Mother for your keep and where is the money coming from?" I said that I would sign on the dole and pay Mother from my unemployment money. I was glad that I was in the hospital when he asked me about coming back to the shop. It meant that he had to answer me without showing how he really felt about my reply in front of strangers. He never once asked how I was like Mother did as soon as they arrived.

A few days later I left the hospital and, having been given the 'all clear', I signed on the dole at the local Labour Exchange. I found it unusual, living at home and not working in the shop, and not having interrupted meals. I decided the best thing was to go out every day for walks in the countryside and keep away from Father. One place I often went to was the main railway line to watch the new diesel engines doing trials, pulling upwards of twelve coaches up the Hemmerton Incline, reputed to be the second steepest incline in the railway network. Prior to these trials, it took two steam engines, either in tandem or one at the front and one at the rear, to get the train up the incline. Needless to say, the diesel engine did it very easily, being much more powerful than the steam engines.

I also saw the start of a new building programme of a new housing estate in the fields where we used to play as small boys.

Frank and Betty were married at St. Mary's Church in May with Betty's father officiating, he being the vicar. The wedding went off very well but there were rumours that Betty was not the kind of girl that she should be, and that the marriage would not last. Frank, to my knowledge, was unaware of this and I, for one, kept my own counsel about what I had heard. They rented a flat in Underwood, which was another part of Plympton.

It was while they were there that Father found out that Frank had been taking tinned food from Father's shop. Father guessed what had been going on when, on a visit to Frank and Betty, he noticed how well stocked they were for tinned food. Father had also been told by Frank's landlord that he was in arrears with his rent. Father arranged to pay the rent owing, on the understanding that Frank would pay him back. Shortly after this, they left Plympton and went to Southsea to live.

Father's sister, Anne, came to stay about a month later. It was now early July and Mother told her of the situation that I was in. Aunt Anne, like Father, was a hard person, but not where I was concerned. She had noticed in her previous visit what Father was like to me. She sized up the situation and asked me when I wanted to leave home. I replied, "Next week", but I said I needed to borrow the fare from Father first, then I would be able to leave home. I never thought of asking Mother for the fare. Aunt Anne gave me the money to book my one-way ticket by coach, which I did without Father knowing. On returning home, at Aunt Anne's bidding, I told Father that I was leaving home and that he owed Aunt Anne £3. He had no option but to pay her and he got the impression that she was against him too.

On the eve of me leaving home I went to one of the local pubs with my friends for a farewell drink. Everything was going well with them wishing me, "Good luck" and saying they admired me for having the guts leaving home for pastures new, when Father walked in. He said I would soon be back home crying in my Mother's apron. Whether or not he said it to encourage me to do well, I shall never know, but my immediate reaction was to say, "I'll prove you bloody well wrong." He then said, "Hark at the beer talking." That nearly started a slanging match between us, so I just said, "Roll on tomorrow," and left the pub with my friends and went to another one.

The next morning Mother did not want to see me go and became emotional, perhaps seeing her youngest son leaving home. I reassured her not to worry as I would be all right staying with Bruce and Celia, Alan and Stephen, and that I would not be completely on my own. I think I said cheerio to Father in the shop beforehand. I caught the 8.00 a.m. coach bound for London and then by the underground train out to Watford.

On reaching Carpender's Park Station I was met by Bruce. We walked to his house, which was about half a mile away, getting in about 8.00 p.m., being greeted by Celia, Alan and Stephen. Now I began to wonder what the next days would be like that lay ahead. First of all, I had to get to know Watford, find out where the Labour Exchange was and get to know my bearings.

* * * *

As you can see, over the years that I lived at home I seem to have given a bad impression of Father and his treatment of me all the time; this is not so. I have tried to be honest about the way that I was treated by him and *not* to sound or be vindictive, but the facts speak for themselves and I think that Father's problem with me was that he could not come to terms with my disability and its expense to him. He also would not believe me on several occasions and I give one example as follows.

Father employed a customer to come in each Thursday evening to clean the counters and wash the shop floor. I was watching her from the kitchen doorway one week and saw her take an ounce of twist tobacco from a drawer and put it in her apron pocket. After she'd left the shop I told Father what I had seen and I said that I would put it down in the book on her list for the end of the week for payment (some customers paid weekly which was entered daily in the book). She denied taking the tobacco, but I argued that she did and after further discussions, Father believed her and not me. I was so upset that I went to the bottom of the staircase and cried my eyes out. Father said to Mother, "What's the matter with him?" Mother replied, "Well if you don't know, you'd better ask him, but for you to believe a liar and not your own son is it any wonder why he is so upset?" I refused to go back into the shop for the rest of the day. The next week the woman said she would not be coming to clean the shop any more, so it was left to me to do it and I was not paid the 2/6d that she was paid.

He was also hard on my brothers during their formative years too, but I felt that I was the one who got it the most.

There was another time while Bruce was serving in the Naval Reserve and on "native" leave that he and Father had, as Bruce would call it, a "heated discussion", and Father would or could not comprehend what Bruce tried to explain. It ended by Bruce leaving home and returning to the naval barracks. The next evening Mother expected Bruce home for tea as usual between 5.00 and 6.00 p.m., but he did not arrive. This went on for a few days when Mother received a letter from him explaining why he was not coming home anymore. Naturally, Mother was very upset about this and she must have replied to his letter, because he came home when he had a day off. Bruce is a great forceful debater and can be very good at explaining his point of view. Perhaps Father may have been jealous of this.

In later years, when any of us had done well, he was very proud of our achievements and he was not afraid to say so. It was by our own efforts that we did this with no help from him.

My relationship with my mother was good in comparison to Father, but as in all walks of life, when a child does any wrong, they are admonished and I had my fair share. I was most annoyed that Mother had kept me in a blouse until well after my fifth birthday. I felt like a sissy and would rather have worn a shirt like the other boys of my age. As I grew older, we got on reasonably well and she could relent or give in to my wishes at times. When I went out, Father would want to know where I was going and why and Mother would tell him sometimes. The main thing that I admired Mother for was how she became the peace maker between Father and me in any arguments and disputes that we had. Very often it was Mother and I versus Father, as the "shop cleaning and tobacco" quote above verifies. Yes, Mother was a friend in many ways, but I felt sorry for her when Father left her on her own after we, as young men, had all gone out as well. I vowed that I would never treat my wife like that if I ever got married.

Chapter Eleven

INTO THE UNKNOWN
AND PASTURES NEW

After I settled in with Bruce and Celia the first thing that I did was to go by bus into Watford and find the Labour Exchange. Bruce had shown me on a map where to get off the bus and find the lane where it was. He bought a local paper with the list of vacancies and, at first, I decided not to look for work in shops. However, money being a scarce commodity in many ways, I would walk rather than spend money on buses, I was then able to afford more cigarettes, and not finding work, it was decided that I had to get a job in a shop to get me started in work again.

I began work in September in a general groceries shop in the High Street called Taylor Brothers. They had several branches throughout the Home Counties. The manager was a short, stout man called Mr. Pratt, who referred to me as a country bumpkin. I learnt quite a lot from him on more aspects of shopkeeping, such as knowing how to cut bacon and the various cuts and joints, and how to cook 14 lb gammon hams, and serving the delicatessen meats that he stocked for the Europeans who lived in Watford.

Also on the staff was a little Irishman who lived on drink rather than food; in consequence, he was a very thin man. Another assistant on the staff was taller than me but full of confidence and he could sell anything to anyone. He delivered the orders to the outlying areas once a week in the firm's van. After I left, I found out that he had done time in a prison.

We had a lady who worked in the office and did the book keeping and took the orders on the phone. She was a lovely lady and I got on well with her. One day, I was told to weigh out a sack of sugar. I was expected to get 113 lbs out of a 112 lbs sack. I told the manager that was impossible, but I was told that the paper bags would allow for it. There were nearly always discrepancies where weighing was concerned and I felt a sense of guilt when doing as the manager expected of the staff.

In the run-up to Christmas we began to get busier each day and we were taking orders for poultry as well as other festive foods. On a very busy Saturday afternoon, Sam Costa (the famous radio personality) and his wife walked in and he expected his wife to be served without waiting. He made himself known to Mr. Pratt, the manager, and asked that his wife should be served without delay. Mr. Pratt replied, "I don't care if your wife is the Queen of England, she will have to wait her turn like anyone else." With that, Sam Costa and his wife left the shop. Mr. Pratt then told us he had observed Sam Costa leaving Sainsbury's shop opposite because they had been kept waiting.

I had ordered a large chicken as a present for Bruce and Celia but we would cook it on New Year's Day, because I was going to spend Christmas at Plympton. Two days before Christmas, a widow customer of ours with two small daughters did not have a chicken for Christmas and Mr. Pratt was very unhelpful. I then offered my chicken to her on the understanding that it could be replaced for me after Christmas. Imagine my horror when Mr. Pratt charged her more than the bird had cost me and I went back to Bruce and Celia and told them what had happened. I was very upset about this and I told Mr. Pratt that he was not being fair to the widow. He just brushed it off and said, "That's what business is all about." I also mentioned it to the clerk and she agreed with me, but she would not discuss it with Mr. Pratt.

I saw to it in future that each time the widow came to the shop each week, I served her myself and under-charged her on all the items that she bought. She gained a lot more from me than the manager took from her with the cost of that chicken at Christmas.

I travelled overnight to Plymouth by train on Christmas Eve and I arrived in Plymouth at 7.00 a.m.. I got a taxi to Plympton and arrived home in time for breakfast. Then I went to bed until about 2.00 p.m.

Father was full of questions on what my job was like and I told him and Mother about the chicken and the widow incident and they could not believe what I told them. I know Father would never have done that to a customer.

While I was home I went to see the friends that I had left behind, but with some of them I got the impression I was not welcome. Perhaps they were jealous that I had made the effort to leave home and they had not.

One evening I got home after seeing some friends about 11.00 p.m. and Father greeted me with, "Where have you been? It's late." I replied, "Father, I am now nearly twenty-six years old and not sixteen." With that I went to bed. Next morning, I told Mother I would not be sorry to get back to Watford, and when she asked me why, I told her what Father had said when I came home the night before. Mother went to Father and said, "Haven't you realised yet that all your sons have grown up and are now all young men?"

I returned to Watford and went back to work, which I was not looking forward to. Mr. Pratt had begun to find fault with me more often than the rest of the staff. The lady in the office noted this and took me aside and advised me to get another job.

The replaced chicken I had expected to be equal in weight to the one the widow had. This was not so - I was given a much smaller chicken and I had no reduction price-wise on it. I vowed I would never trust that manager ever again.

* * * *

Early in January 1953, the district manager, with whom I got on well, offered me a manager's position in Kenton, North London, which I accepted. I had one member of staff to help me and my first job was to dispose of three crates of rotten eggs. They had come from a packing shed in Suffolk. I tried to claim on the loss but I was not successful.

After taking over the shop, travelling to Kenton by train and bus was a nightmare for me and I could never guarantee getting there on time to open the shop, which I was concerned about, and it was always very late in the evenings by the time that I got back to Bruce and Celia's. Celia never knew what time I would get back so my evening meal was kept warm for me. At least I was away from Mr. Pratt.

While I was at Kenton the van at Watford with the orders on it was stopped by the Weights and Measures Government Department. It was found that in almost all the orders there were discrepancies in the weights and prices. The van and its contents were impounded and the driver and manager were summonsed to appear in court in Watford. The driver's past history came out and that's when we found out about his previous convictions. As a result, both men were sacked by the firm and new staff were employed.

I next got myself employed by the Watford Co-Operative Society in North Watford. This shop had the old fashioned cups suspended by wires to the accounts office so that when you put the cash in these cups, a lever was pulled and the cup went along at great speed above the customers' heads. The cup was returned by the same method with the change and receipt inside.

The one job I hated doing was skinning 20 lb or 30 lb cheeses to get the cheese cloth off prior too cutting it into various wedges for the display counter.

One week, the manager had been to Manchester to see the C.W.S. factories making biscuits and other items of food which they manufactured. The next week, during a morning coffee break, he spoke highly of the quantity of biscuits being produced. I retorted that they would not compare with the quality produced by the other well-known private manufacturers, of which there were many in those days, such as Huntley and Palmers, Jacobs, McVitie and Price, and Crawfords, to name but a few.

The next thing I knew was, on returning after work to Bruce and Celia's on the Saturday evening about 7.00 p.m., there was a letter for me from the Co-Op head office, telling me that my services were no longer required and that the following Saturday I was to collect my cards and any due wages at 6.30 p.m. from the company office. Bruce and Celia were as surprised as I was but I put it down to my comments about quality rather than quantity, and the manager had reported me. I found this to be true when I collected my cards.

It was during this year that I joined the Young Conservatives in my spare time. Bruce and Celia said I needed to join something besides just going to the cinema and Sunday afternoon walks with Bruce and my nephews, Alan and Stephen.

The Y.C.s, as they were known, were all of my own age group and I soon got to know them well. The persons I really got on well with were Peter Eames, who was the leader of the dance band, Bettine, a school teacher, Hunter Mitchell and Tony Philpot.

On one of our evenings together, Peter, Tony and I were at Peter's house when we recorded an hour of anything we could think of with the piano, recitations, songs incorrectly sung, interspersed with jokes. The tape recorder was one of the first ones that I had ever seen with very large reels of tape. The result was not very good. Tony went on to become a sound engineer with the B.B.C.. He is still there and is now in a senior position.

I don't know what became of Peter Eames, but Hunter and Bettine got married and had five children. They still live in St. Albans and are now grandparents.

The Y.C.s held a dance every four weeks in Bushey, which always had a theme to decorate the hall. Another member that I was introduced to was Doreen Luck and my West Country accent seemed to amuse her. We soon realised that we had a lot in common in likes and dislikes. She lived at the bottom of the road where I was staying with Bruce and Celia. She was a librarian in Boots the Chemist's library department, further down the High Street from where I was working.

We began going out together and she gave me a lot of encouragement in trying to improve my station in life. As a consequence, we found new digs in Bushey for me, which Bruce and Celia were pleased about because it meant they had more room for themselves. At that time, Alan suffered very badly with asthma and it was not until he began wearing long trousers that he showed any real signs of improvement in his condition. When Mother heard from me that I had moved into new digs, she was disturbed, asking if Bruce and I had fallen out with each other. I had to write back and tell her that we had an understanding between us that, as soon as I was all right with a job, I would look for other digs because their council house only had two bedrooms. I believe Bruce wrote to Mother at the same time and explained what we had agreed between us. This put Mother's mind at rest and as I wrote to her every week, she knew that I went to see Bruce and Celia most weeks.

The people I stayed with were Mr. and Mrs. Bradley, two retired nurses from Shenley Mental Hospital. When they wanted to use the bathroom, Mr. and Mrs. Bradley had to pass by the foot of my bed in my bedroom to get to it. Her cooking was not up to much, mostly stodgy food and no variety. If I left any food on my plate, she always asked, "What's up, don't you like my cooking?" I used the excuse that I was not very hungry having been eating at work. I soon left there and went back to Watford to live in digs with another retired couple, and only five minutes walk from the shop.

Mr. and Mrs. Sears made me feel at home and very welcome, he was a real Cockney and could talk in the Cockney rhyming slang. They had two married daughters who lived in other parts of Watford. The backdoor of their house was not accessible from the road, so I had to take my cycle through the house to put it away out in the shed. I had arranged to get my bicycle sent to Watford from Plympton.

When we had the General Election, I stayed with Bruce until 3.00 a.m. listening to the results before going back to my digs. Getting my cycle through the house disturbed Mr. Sears and he told me off next day for waking him up. I think the Election result upset him as well.

Early in July, I went to Plympton for a week's holiday, in which some relations expected me to visit them, but I just wanted to be home for my break and not travel to other towns.

It was during this week that Father was made a very good offer for the shop and sub-post office by a prospective buyer. I went out to the cinema in Plymouth while this was going on. On my return, Father had gone to one of his Masonic meetings, so I asked Mother what had happened about the prospective buyer, and Mother replied that Father had turned his offer down. She explained the offer to me and I said, "Father must be daft to turn down such a good offer."

After Mother had gone to bed, Father came home and I asked him what had happened about the shop. He said that he had turned the offer down. When I asked, "Why?", he said, "The offer was £2,000 deposit with seven years to pay off the balance plus rent and rates." I explained to Father that he would not get a better offer on those terms, money at that time was very short due to the economic situation. I also reminded him of what he had told me about his health and that he and Mother were not getting any younger, his words not mine. This discussion went on until nearly 2.00 a.m., when we both went to bed.

The next morning, I got up late and I heard Father on the phone having a long discussion. Mother greeted me with, "What did you say to your Father last night?" I told her that I had a long talk with him about selling the shop, she replied that he was now talking to his solicitor trying to re-open the negotiations with the prospective buyer. Mother was pleased that I had talked to Father and got him to change his mind. By the 1st of September he had sold the business and the new owner, Mr. Newton, had taken over.

At the end of my week at home I returned to Watford and I brought my collection of 78 rpm records with me.

My next job was with a husband and wife team that ran a grocery shop in Radlett, about five miles from Watford. The husband and I did not get on too well and he was often blaming my disability if he thought I was not pulling my weight. His wife, on the other hand, had the opposite attitude towards me. I tried to reason with him at times, but to no avail.

I continued working there under this strain until early in the New Year.

Chapter Twelve

A NEW JOB AND A BROAD EXPERIENCE

Early in January 1954, I went into hospital for the amputation of my little toe on my right foot, which I had been walking on because it was bent under my foot. Each morning after the operation, the beds were stripped and remade. One morning, the nurse asked me if I was decent, I said, "Of course I am," and with that the nurse flung all the bed clothes off me where I was lying naked as the day I was born. I was not covered by the modesty sheet and that's what the nurse had meant by decent, so hospitals have their lighter moments.

Soon after that, whilst still a patient, I saw in the local paper that my job at the shop was advertised. When I was discharged from the hospital I went to the shop in Radlett to find out what was going on. I was given a week's salary and my employment cards and told that I was no longer needed.

From there, I went to see Bruce and Celia. I had already made arrangements to stay with Frank in Southsea for a few days. My visit to Frank was not a good idea. His relationship with his wife was very strained and he seldom, if ever, came home early from work. Frank and I were all right to each other but we had very little time together. He had to get his own meals after leaving work so he was too tired for entertaining me.

On my return to Watford I soon got myself another job, this time with the Maypole Co. in the High Street, who were by then part of Allied Suppliers Ltd., which included such famous names as Liptons and Home and Colonial Stores. Mr. Wilkinson was a good manager and after I had been there for six months, I was made first assistant, in other words deputy manager. We got on well together, bouncing ideas off each other in trying to increase the turnover. I was in charge of the staff and we had full and part-time women and young girls working with us. Quite a lot of leg-pulling went on but it was all done in good fun.

We had to deal with company representatives and one or two I knew from working with Father. They had been transferred to new areas and were surprised to see me in Watford.

We had to introduce a new product called 'May Queen' margarine which had 10% butter in it. Food rationing was still in force on some food items so this was a feature to try and get the customers to buy more margarine.

On one Sunday each month I went to Hounslow to visit Aunt Anne, who always cooked me a lovely roast dinner.

Not long after I first met Doreen, her father died and I was due for my usual Sunday visit to see Aunt Anne. I had managed to get Doreen invited, so we went two days after her father's funeral. Doreen was a little subdued when we first met that morning on the train to London, but she did ask me questions about Aunt Anne, what was she like, etc.. I warned her that Aunt Anne would dominate any conversation that we would have. We got to Aunt Anne's all right and after the introductions, we sat down to lunch. Aunt Anne, true to form, did most of the talking as I had forecast, and when she was in full flow, you could not get a word in.

She told Doreen all about the family on Father's side and she was not too complimentary about some of them. I quite thought Doreen would be bored with the family history so I was glad when we had to take our leave shortly after tea and get the train into London, then back to Watford. Walking to the station, I began to apologise to Doreen, but she burst out laughing. So I said, "What's the joke?" and she replied, "You are a good talker, Norman, but you'll have to go a long way to beat your Aunt Anne; you could not get a word in edgeways." Then she went on to say, "Who does she remind you of?" and I replied that I did not know. She then said, "Joyce Grenfell," and then began to mimic Aunt Anne. We both laughed at this and when we got back to her house, she could not thank me enough. The day had been such a great success for her that she was able to forget for a few hours what she had recently been through.

Life continued normally for the rest of the year. Doreen, who by now had known Bruce and Celia for quite some time, looked after Alan and Stephen some evenings until Bruce arrived home from work. Celia had a part-time job as an usherette at the Palace Theatre. Gwen Watford and Jimmy Perry were two of the resident actors there at the time. I went to see some of the plays and I was amazed to find out that, while they acted one week, during the day they rehearsed the next week's play while reading through the script of the next play. Very good training, I would think. Also in my spare time, I was very active with the Young Conservatives, organising dances and other social events such as rambles on Sunday afternoons; and the year ended with house parties.

After some dances we used to get into cars and go to an all night transport café on the Watford bypass and have a fry up supper of bacon and eggs, fried bread and chips.

At about this time, we had a new member who had joined us called John Beales, who was a medical student. Hunter and I made good friends with him and we became a trio. We went around quite a lot together and sometimes Bettine came along as well.

In late summer Doreen went to Brighton for two weeks' holiday and we arranged that I would go to Brighton on Saturday evening after work. I got to Brighton about 9.00 p.m. and gave Doreen the parcel of clean clothes she had asked me to bring down from her mother. We spent the weekend together and she asked me to come down again the following weekend, which I did. Brighton did not agree with me and the sea air made me feel drowsy, so I never wanted to go there again.

Bruce, Celia and I had been discussing a holiday together on the Norfolk Broads in the summer. Bruce did all the booking arrangements for July and we had a chalet by the riverside near Potter Heigham. I then began to save up for the holiday because we were going by train to get there, which was quite an expense. I had difficulty getting the Saturday off at the start of my holiday, so a compromise was arranged. We all took our holidays during the summer taking it in seniority, and we had a temporary manager for two weeks while Mr. Wilkinson was away.

I went on the Norfolk Broads as arranged with Bruce, Celia and Alan and Stephen. With the chalet that we hired was a small dinghy which was powered by an outboard motor. We made use of it most days but we were not very good with it.

On our return from the Broads we witnessed a boat catching fire and it was burnt out. On our journey to London, the train was delayed in a tunnel for an hour or more outside Liverpool Street Station on that very hot summer Saturday and we nearly got dehydrated. We managed to buy some cold drinks before getting the train back to Watford. We would not like to have that experience again.

In the autumn, we experienced the worst smog on record which lasted several days. After leaving work one evening at 5.45 p.m., it took me three hours to get home to Oxhey estate by bus, with the conductor walking in front of the bus guiding the driver. It was the same next morning trying to get to work, when literally everyone was late or did not get to work.

At the same time, there was the Lynton and Lynmouth flood disaster in North Devon with many lives lost, and thousands of pounds of damage. Not a very good start to the winter months.

At the shop one day I found a 10/- note in a fixture under the counter in amongst the bags of sugar. I gave it to the manager and told him where I had found it. He kept all the staff in after the shop closed and told them what I had found; he wanted the culprit to own up and then he would decide what action to take. No one owned up so we all went home. Next morning, we had one member of staff who did not turn up, so we guessed it was she who had stolen the money. A few days went by and the next thing we heard was that she had applied for a job in our St. Albans' branch because the manager phoned our manager for a reference. Needless to say, she did not get the job.

At our branch we were short staffed and to help ourselves, I suggested stripping out the window on Saturday nights instead of Monday mornings. So we tried this and by 10.00 a.m. on Monday we had cleaned and redressed the shop window. The consequent result was that we nearly doubled our Monday takings. This continued for some weeks until the head office phoned the manager and asked him how we had made the increased takings on the Mondays. He explained about the staff shortages and told him of my idea about clearing out the window on Saturdays and cleaning and redressing on Mondays. They said what a good idea and adopted it throughout the company. The reward I got was to be offered the managership of the St. Albans' branch.

I began to work in St. Albans with a staff of two part-time ladies; one came in the mornings and the other in the afternoons. The stock was several hundreds of pounds in the red when I took over. In the cellar under the shop was a curved area under the pavement which was full of empty biscuit tins. I sent those back to the depot and the boxes of dried fruit that I found I transferred to my old branch in Watford, where I knew they would be sold. There was other stock I was able to get moved as well, the amount of stock being far too great for the amount of the turnover from the customers. I had found the missing stock, but to do it I was working seven days a week at no extra payment. My wages were now £7 10/- per week gross as manager.

I was asked to get digs in St. Albans but I refused, and after I had been there for three months, the district manager became awkward towards me, so much so that one Monday morning I saw him waiting for me. As soon as he saw me, he hid around the corner until I approached the shop door with my keys at the ready to open the door. He greeted me with, "Good morning, I see that you are late opening the shop. Is there any reason for this?" I said, "If you must know, I was here until late on Saturday evening and again yesterday, stock-taking, so I overslept this morning, and it is far better to be late than not to arrive at all." Needless to say, my answer did not go down very well with him and shortly after this, I was transferred back to the Watford branch, where I stayed until the early autumn.

Mrs. Sears' son-in-law, Eric, worked at the British American Optical Factory and he knew that I was looking to change my present job. I was tired of having to work the long hours and all day Saturdays, and holidays could not start until after 5.30 p.m.

on that day; besides, I wanted more money than £6 a week, my wages having been reduced after leaving St. Albans. He told me there would be a vacancy at the Factory after the annual holiday shutdown and that he'd had a word with the foreman. I applied for the vacancy and went for the interview and got the job at £10 per five day week, Monday to Friday.

I had booked a holiday in Switzerland and I was going with a new girl friend called Audrey. It was her intention to renew a friendship with a Swiss boy whom she had met the previous year. By now, Doreen and I were still friends but very much independent of each other.

I spent a week in Interlaken and I made visits to other parts of the country while I was there, crossing Lake Thun and going to Grindlewald and Berne. Audrey spent a day going to see the Swiss boy, but he spurned her and she returned to Interlaken in tears. I then had to comfort her and try to get her to forget all about him. By the next day she had recovered so it was not all that serious.

On our return to England I left Audrey with her mother at Victoria Station and I crossed over to Paddington Station where I caught the afternoon train to Plymouth. I did this to please Father because he remarked to Aunt Enid and Uncle Bill that I should have gone home to see Mother and him and not go to Switzerland. Uncle Bill and Aunt Enid told me about this next time I saw them. They had told Father, "Good luck to Norman; we are pleased that he is doing well and able to travel to other countries."

On my return to Watford a week later, I returned to work and I handed in my week's notice to the shop manager. He thought I had more potential in the shop business and that I was doing wrong moving on. However, he wished me the best of luck when I left.

What a difference factory work was compared to being in a shop. The first thing that I noticed was that it was a lot noisier with the machinery working, but we did have 'Music While You Work' twice a day, relayed over the tannoy system, which put us in a good frame of mind. My job was making the brass gauges that gauged the curves of the moulds which ground down the lenses; I had to correct any that were worn down or make new ones. This meant I had the freedom to walk all over the factory to all the sections and departments, so I was able to see how lenses were manufactured from a large sheet of glass down to the finished lens.

Christmas was approaching and it was on a Thursday this year, this meant that we would get four if not five consecutive days off. I was invited to stay because Mr. and Mrs. Sears' families were planning to celebrate the season with a big party. In all, we were seven adults and five children. We started on Christmas Day with the turkey meal and all the trimmings, followed by the pudding and crackers. It was then time for the presents to be opened. After that, we played games with the children, then went on to card games. The beer was plentiful but no one ever over-indulged. This went on until about 4.00 a.m. and the next morning we went to one of the daughter's houses and carried on as before. We finished about 2.00 a.m., this time the children getting very tired much sooner than before.

The next day it was off to the other daughter's house after lunch and again we had plenty to eat and drink; this went on again until about 4.00 a.m. In all, it was one of the most memorable Christmas periods that I have ever had. No one got the worse for drink, it was just like a great big happy family party. We had a similar party on New Year's Eve but we had to go to work the next day.

Eric had a motorbike and sidecar and early one Sunday, he took me on the pillion to see the famous Sunday Petticoat Lane market in London. On nearing the market, I noticed a shop with the sign above it with the name Dunkley and I could not help thinking they may have been a relation. On the return journey back to Watford I insisted on riding in the sidecar. My reason was that I could not keep my right foot on the footrest each time we went over a bump in the road. We still got back in time for lunch at 1.30 p.m.

I had now been at the Factory for six months and three weeks before Christmas we had a tragedy there.

Behind the Factory was the single main line to St. Albans from Watford Junction Station and on this day, just after lunch, I went to the men's toilet. While I was there I spoke to some of the men who were there, mainly about how much time we were going to get off for Christmas and how we were going to celebrate the festive season.

One man in the group broke a Factory rule, with another person, and at about 4.30 p.m. went to the shops in St. Albans Road via the rail track at the back of the Factory, then down from the track into the road by the railway bridge. On their return by the same route one of them was knocked down and killed by the train which had just left the station for St. Albans at 4.50 p.m.

At the inquest it was stated that they did not hear the train approaching them. The accident really shook everyone in the Factory and the rear of the Factory was barred to everyone from then on. A sad end to the year for all of us.

*   *   *   *

After the Christmas holiday break we went back to work in the hope that the New Year of 1956 would be a better one.

Mr. and Mrs. Sears wanted me to leave them. Their reason was that he had not been too well lately and she needed more time to look after him. I managed to find myself a bedsit in Gammons Lane which was not too far away from the Factory. There was a lady dietician from the hospital in the top two rooms and I had the ground floor front room.

Very soon after moving in I had to have a cyst removed from my left foot which was being aggravated by the shoe laces. Because there was no sick pay, I had to return to work after the operation, which was done in the hospital out-patients department under a local anaesthetic.

Back at the digs the dietician and I did not like the arrangement of a shared bathroom with the family of six who lived there, or the conditions of the house, so with her help I put an advert. in the local press under a box number. The present landlady replied to my advert. along with three others. The dietician left soon after and a Nigerian rented her rooms; his cooking smelt throughout the whole house of spices and garlic. I replied to two answers that I had. The first one wanted me to only use the rear entrance and to remove my footwear before entering the kitchen. I explained to the lady that this was impossible for me to do because, with my foot, I had to keep my shoes on for the support that my foot required. The so-called front lounge was cluttered up with furniture and bric-a-brac with hardly any room to relax in.

I then went to the other house in the same avenue and it happened to be opposite the other one. Here I felt at home right away; the owners were a Mrs. Baker and her sister, Miss Edwards. Hunter had a car so, with his help, I moved to No. 108 Oxhey Avenue as soon as I could. There were two other lodgers, one Mr. Walsh, who was retired, and another man who worked for a national tyre company. We all got on well together, even to the point of watching TV on Sunday evenings together. Mr. Walsh went to the local pub on Watford Heath most evenings.

The other man left because he was getting married, so his room was let to a retired soldier who had been an officer. He had a very bad bronchial chest and he would not go and see a doctor. Eventually, one Saturday, Mrs. Baker made him promise that he would go to see the doctor on the Monday. The next morning, Sunday, he came up the stairs and went into the bathroom. After a few minutes we heard a big thump in the bathroom and we knocked on the door and called out to him, but we got no reply. We tried to open the door but he was against it. We then decided that Mr. Walsh would call the fire brigade. A fireman looked into the bathroom window and saw that Mr. Saunders was slumped against the door. The fireman climbed in through the window and managed to get him away from the door and take him to his room and laid him on his bed. He was dead and we had to call the doctor to certify this. Mrs. Baker decided not to take another lodger, so Mr. Walsh and I were the only ones left.

Sam Costa lived in the same avenue and we often saw him going down the avenue on his way to London to record 'Much Binding in the Marsh'. Several radio and TV personalities lived in the area but their names escape me now.

Mr. Walsh and Mrs. Baker between them decided to rent an allotment behind the back garden of the house. They set to work tidying up the ground and preparing it for the vegetables that they intended to grow. After work I used to help them in the evenings. What Mr. Walsh hated was after all the hard work he had put in, to see his marrows had been stolen. They had been grown on a mound of soil which he had prepared very carefully to get the best results. However, we did get the other vegetables and salad crops all right and I picked up many tips which I was able to use in later years.

After another season they gave it up, mainly because the salad crops and vegetables had been either stolen or vandalised.

I was still seeing John Beales whenever he was home at weekends from the hospital where he worked, and Hunter and Bettine. About once a month, on a Saturday evening, we would all go out to a restaurant in the country and have an evening three course meal. One meal that I had was porterhouse steak and it really filled my plate. Anyway, I did not let it beat me and I ate the lot, a most enjoyable evening out.

When John qualified as a doctor in medicine, he completed his year as a houseman in a hospital and then he was called up into the Army to do two years' service. He was eventually sent to Singapore, where he stayed until he returned to England and was then discharged.

We were still having the Y.C. dances once a month and on one such night we had a nautical theme complete with ship's wheel and mock-up bridge. I was the M.C. for that evening and one spot we had was Peter Eames giving his interpretation of a selection of some light classical music played in the modern idiom. After the dance was over we went back to a member's house where we had supper and Peter entertained us again at the piano. It was early Sunday morning before any of us got home after having had such a good time. We were often invited to various members' houses for social gatherings and suppers which were all very enjoyable, a good time being had by all.

One member called Christine and I had the same birthday so when this piece of useless information leaked out, we were called the twins from then on by the other members.

Work continued at the Factory and one young chap called Vincent asked me if I would make up a party of six to hire a boat on the Norfolk Broads. I went to my digs and gave it some thought. I discussed it with Bruce and Celia on my next visit to them. We worked out how much it would cost, plus spending money to see if I could afford it. When I returned to work I had another talk with Vincent before I committed myself to such a venture. I did agree to go and we had to book a car to get us to Acle, our pickup point for the boat; we also hired the car to bring us back to Watford the following weekend as none of us could drive.

We had about half an hour's tuition on the rudiments of the boat and how to fill it up with oil and petrol and the River Code, which is opposite to that for the roads.

We made our way towards Norwich, taking it in turns to steer the boat. On our way back towards Great Yarmouth, we got the boat stuck on the mud bank and we had to send to the boat yard for help getting us off the bank. While we were waiting we found it very strange to walk on the deck with the boat leaning to starboard at an acute angle. We were marooned for several hours because we also had to wait for the tide to rise so that it would help in freeing the boat. We eventually got to Great Yarmouth in the evening and decided to go into the town and have a fish and chip supper. About four of the lads managed to get friendly with four girls and invited them back to the boat. It meant that I and one other stayed on the deck for most of the night while the others were having a good time below.

When we got back to Watford I told Vincent that if he intended going again another year, I would not be going. He and some of the others got drunk on barley wine which I never drank. I only drank ordinary mild or bitter beer. In those days there were no cans of beer available. On reflection, that was a blessing in disguise.

Work continued after the holiday and it was just normal working. I tried nearly every week to get overtime on a Saturday morning so that I would get more money, but the foreman turned it down most weeks.

I usually wrote home every week but there were times when there was nothing to write home about so I would leave it. When this happened the first time, Mother wrote and asked me why had I not written. I wrote and explained that there was no news to tell her that week, and I might miss writing the odd week and she was not to worry.

Socially, things could not be better, with dances and parties, and for over a year I had been going to the town hall once a month to the concerts by the London Philharmonic Orchestra. I quite enjoyed them and there was always a not so well known piece played as well as the popular ones. It gave me something else to look forward to each month and, of course, it broadened my liking for more of the classical kind of music.

Christmas and the New Year came and went and in my spare time, I went to many dances and parties during that period and generally I was having a good time.

Interlude

Above; Forder Gardens 1927. Mother at back. Front left to right, Father, myself, Ron, Frank, Bruce, with Jack Collier just visible at rear. Left, part of the choir of St Maurice's Church: clockwise from top; Ron, Frank, myself, and Bruce, August 4th 1937.

Top pictures; Forder Gardens gatehouse today, and below the Forder Gardens gardeners, about 1910. My maternal grandfather, Frederick Joseph Collier is on the left, with his sons (my uncles) Harold and Charlie, with William on the right.

*Left; effigy of St Maurice in the
church named after him in
Plympton.
Above, memorial to Sir Joshua
Reynolds in the same church.
Below; Father outside his
shop, before the post office was
added.*

Top pictures; my wedding to Margaret, 6th August 1960.
Above; family group showing, from left, my mother,
Dr John Beales, neice Janet, myself, Margaret, Olive
and Margaret's parents.

Top picture; "The Three Must Get Beers"
From left, Frank, myself and Bruce, 1949
Above; Family group, Christmas 1965.
From left, John, Margaret, Andrew and myself.

Above; Family group on holiday at Portland Bill.
From left; Andrew, myself, Kenneth, Margaret and John.

Margaret, Stourport, 15th July 1992

Family group at our pearl wedding celebrations, showing, from left, John, myself, Andrew, Margaret and Kenneth.

PART TWO

1957 - 1993

Chapter Thirteen

ROMANCE BLOSSOMS

1957 was very uneventful to start with and life just went on as normal. We got beyond the spring and summer when we had rambles, or went out on Sundays in cars and travelled around the countryside visiting various villages.

I had decided to visit Mother and Father for Christmas so I travelled down by train as usual to Plympton, but I was not feeling very well. I returned to Watford on Boxing Day still not feeling too good, being bent double in pain.

Mr. Walsh went and phoned for the doctor and when he arrived, he could hardly walk himself. He had strained a muscle in his back. I had got orchitis, which needed hospital treatment. As the doctor got up to leave he said, "What with your testicles and my bad back, we make a brilliant pair." Mr. Walsh and I burst out laughing, but I was too embarrassed to tell Miss Edwards when she enquired what Mr. Walsh and I were laughing at. I was admitted to hospital in Watford where I was examined and told to drink as much fruit juice and water as possible. This was to flush out the infection.

I was first examined by a houseman doctor and then the consultant came to see me. This was Mr. Loosemore, whom I recognised at once. After reading my name and notes, he said to me, "Your name seems familiar," and I said, "Yes, I have served you in my Father's shop at Plympton many times." He replied,

"Of course, your Father is a Councillor on the Plympton Rural District Council," of which Mr. Loosemore's father was the Clerk. When news of this reached Father he was pleased about it and spoke to Mr. Loosemoor Senior about my meeting his son.

Also on that first evening the night nurses arrived on duty and a staff nurse came to make my bed and to check that I was all right, which was followed by a hot drink. This was Staff Nurse Sharp and, of course, I could not resist making remarks about "seeing the point" and "getting the needle". I was smitten by her soon after seeing her for the first time and each night for the rest of my stay in hospital I looked forward to seeing Staff Nurse Sharp. I found out her Christian name was Margaret. Before I was discharged I had arranged a date with her and I gave her my address. It was now January 1958.

Not long after I left hospital I returned to work at the Factory and eventually Margaret and I met for our first date outside the hospital. After that first date we met outside the nurses' home at the rear of the hospital.

At first we began seeing each other as much as possible and we spent most of the time walking in Casiobury Park, which was next to the hospital, getting to know each other. I learnt that she lived in Radlett, which is about five miles from Watford. One day she told me that she had to visit her mother because she had not been home for sometime. Before meeting me she spent the majority of her off-duty time at home. Her mother asked why she had not been home lately, but I don't think that Margaret mentioned me as being the reason at first. Because her mother expected her home more often, we had to compromise when we could meet, but when she was on night duty this was not possible. Margaret lived in the hospital in the nurses' quarters so she had no travelling as such to do. She had passed her S.R.N. exam in late 1957 and was planning to start her midwifery course when a vacancy became available. Margaret wanted to go to The British Hospital for Mothers and Babies in Woolwich, South-East London, but the waiting list for training was long. In the meantime, she carried on nursing at Watford.

The first two films that we saw together were "Bridge on the

River Kwai" and "High Society", two films of the day which were very enjoyable.

I had already introduced her to Bruce and Celia and to everyone at Mrs. Baker's house in Oxhey Avenue.

Miss Edwards, after seeing Margaret a few times with me, passed the remark that we were made for each other. How true this was to be in the future, but we did not take it seriously at the time.

In June, Bruce and Celia moved to Billericay to their bungalow which they had bought, this meant that I was on my own now, but at least Margaret and I were seeing each other and, of course, Bettine, Hunter and Dr. John whenever we could.

Margaret's father was a priest in holy orders but he lived in Shiraz in Persia, working for the Christian Mission Society. He had charge of many churches there which he had designed and had built. He was also a specialist in the Persian languages and he spoke French and German, as well as English. Her mother was a doctor and a J.P. and she went to Shiraz to stay with him nearly every year.

It was not until July that I was invited to meet Margaret's mother, by which time Margaret and I were getting very serious with each other. We went by bus to Radlett together and I was introduced to Margaret's older sister, Olive, as well. She, like John Beales, was a medical student in London. I was then invited to stay to supper. Until then supper to me meant a cup of hot drink and a few biscuits or a piece of toast. Not so at Margaret's house. This was to be a three course meal and as I had already eaten a large meal at my lodgings, I struggled to get through.

Margaret's mother asked me quite a lot about myself and I answered her as best I could. Inwardly, I knew if I intended to marry Margaret, I would have to give a good account of myself. Margaret had to get back to the hospital, so we left Radlett together and went back to Watford.

Her father was due home for two months' holiday in August, so we decided to wait until then before telling them of our plan to get engaged. Margaret had already told her sister Olive and to keep it a secret. We had been discussing getting married, but we decided to wait until Margaret had passed her midwifery course before doing so.

When her father did come home, he nearly always walked with her to the bus stop after her evening visit. I had been going to Radlett to travel back with her, but on this occasion, when I was waiting for her, they walked past me as if I was a total stranger. This was the first time that I had seen her father and I could not understand why Margaret did not introduce me to him. Until then Margaret had never mentioned to him that she had a boy friend, so he was unaware of my existence.

Margaret also had a younger brother called Hugh, who worked for the De-Haviland aircraft company in London Colney, which is situated halfway between Radlett and St. Albans.

At the end of August I was invited to Sunday lunch and to meet the whole family, which included Mrs. Sharp's brother, Raymond. After lunch, Olive was told by both of us that I was going to tell her father that I wanted to marry Margaret. Olive was delighted and became an ally in support of us. I spoke to Mr. Sharp for about ten minutes and he agreed and gave his permission. I then went to find Margaret, who was alone in the lounge, and afterwards we told Olive and she was very pleased with our news.

Mrs. Sharp invited me to stay to tea and we went to evensong together at Christ Church, Radlett, where Olive was in the choir. Shortly after getting back from the service it was time for Margaret and I to leave to catch the bus and return to Watford. As we went through the kitchen, Olive called out, "Good luck for next weekend!" whereupon her mother asked Olive what was that for. She replied, "They are getting engaged next Saturday." Mrs. Sharp was taken by surprise at this news. Apparently, Mr. Sharp had not said anything to Mrs. Sharp about my asking him for Margaret's hand in marriage.

Next Saturday, September 6th, we left Watford early and went by the underground train to London. We found the engagement ring that Margaret wanted and we went into Green Park, where I placed it on her finger. We had lunch and then went to the Whitehall Theatre, where we saw Brian Rix in the farce

"Reluctant Heroes". From there, we went back to Watford and went to the weekly townhall dance. It was adjacent to the hospital so it was not far for Margaret to get to the nurses' quarters. That was a very happy day for both of us to remember for many years to come.

The next morning, she went home for the day and I had to be content with being on my own in Watford. I would much rather have spent the whole day with Margaret. We had arranged that I would call for her in the evening. I went and called at the house as arranged when I knew Margaret would soon be leaving to return to Watford. Olive answered the door and invited me in. Then I met Margaret's parents again. Olive was pleased for both of us and wished us every happiness, her parents politely wished us both good luck and we then left for Watford.

In late-September her father went back to Shiraz and he was not to come home again for several years. Mrs. Sharp was making arrangements to visit him the following year, and then go on to the Holy Land before coming home.

We continued to see each other as and when Margaret was off duty, and we often had tea in the Odeon cinema restaurant if we were going there to see a film. Margaret worked over the Christmas and New Year period, so I had to be content with spending most of the festive season at my digs with Mr. Walsh and Mrs. Baker.

Margaret began her training as a midwife in March 1959, the first six months to be spent at the hospital in Woolwich. She went by train from Radlett to get there, so we were going to be apart very often for the year or maybe longer. We kept in touch by public phone and by writing to each other, and we met as often as possible in London. This was great for me because I got to know the underground railway very well and Margaret and I began to see some of the West End shows. When we saw "My Fair Lady", Margaret had taken her first part midwifery exam earlier that day and she did pass it, so it was a celebration for her to relax and see a good show.

If we were in London on a Sunday we would often go to the evening service at St. Martin's in the Fields Church. Sometimes I went to Woolwich to meet her and take her back from London, but that depended mostly on the trains. Train services were very often disrupted with mainly maintenance work on Sundays.

There was one occasion on a Sunday when I decided that we should go to St Bride's Church in Fleet Street, where I introduced her to the Rev. Cyril Armitage, the senior vicar. He had been a regular customer in Father's shop while I was working there in the early 1940s. Shortly after that meeting in Fleet Street I lost touch with him.

We had arranged a holiday together between the first and second parts of her training. We had booked a bed-and-breakfast for three days in Paignton and the rest of the week we would stay in Plympton. While in Paignton we went to Cockington Village and I also took Margaret to meet Uncle Bill and Aunt Enid in Newton Abbot. While on a beach in Torquay we bought a tray of tea and I tripped over carrying it and spilt the boiling water over Margaret's arm. I took Margaret to a chemist as quickly as I possibly could and got it dressed; luckily it did not leave a scar after it healed. This event upset me a great deal and it concerned me for quite some time. We went on to Plympton and Mother had arranged a bed-and-breakfast in Longbrooke Street for Margaret. She was made to feel very welcome there as everyone liked her right away.

I took Margaret to Bovisands Bay by bus the long way round where we spent the day bathing. I did not bathe very much, but Margaret did quite a lot. We also met my cousin, June, and her family as well as meeting Winnie and her husband, Joe.

On our return from Bovisands, Father asked Margaret his usual question, "Did she see the sea plane?" Margaret replied, "No, but I saw the plain sea!" I had warned Margaret in advance that she would be asked this question. Father looked at me and said, "I suppose you told Margaret," I said, "Yes, I did." He liked to think he could pull anyone's leg, but he did not like it when we caught him out. Except for the accident in Torquay we had a lovely holiday together.

In September, she began working in the district of Woolwich, doing home visits to expectant mothers. She used a very old model of a cycle to get around, and she was on call just like a doctor.

In October, Hunter and Bettine were getting married the weekend that summer time ended. I travelled by coach overnight on Friday to Manchester arriving very early. I sought out a barber's shop for a shave and brush up and I was asked if I had come to see the match. I said, "What match?" and then I was told there was a big football match on that day. I then told the man that I had come up for the wedding.

Travelling back after the wedding the coach driver had to stop for an extra hour because of the time change and it made a long night much longer. I went to Watford and slept for most of the day. In the evening I went to Radlett and travelled with Margaret as far as Waterloo Station where she caught the train to Woolwich, and I returned to Watford.

On Christmas Day I phoned Margaret as arranged and she told me that very early that morning, she had delivered a mother of a 12 pound baby, the heaviest in the district for years. She sounded very proud of achieving this while in training.

Chapter Fourteen

A WEDDING
& A NEW FAMILY

1960 was going to be very important to us both in many ways as, when the year started, Margaret and I knew that in a few short months, we were to be married. But first there was quite a lot for us to do. We had decided that if our marriage was to succeed, we would have to leave Watford and Radlett and start our life together without being influenced by relations.

Early in the New Year, Margaret took her final exams to qualify as a midwife. It would be a month or so before the results were known. Margaret had earlier told me that she had to pay to enter all her nursing exams which I was appalled to hear. Nurses' pay even then was very low so I considered it unfair that they had to pay to enter their exams. When she heard that she had passed her final and had qualified we celebrated it together before she went home to Radlett.

For my part I took time off from work for three days in February and I went to Salisbury to look for work. This was part of our plans for when we were married. I managed to get several interviews and I did like the city, but I was not successful in getting a job. I returned to Watford and I phoned Margaret to let her know how I had got on. At my lodgings there was a letter from Mother telling me that Father was not very well and that he might not live much longer, but there was no need to come home just yet. I then went to Swindon and I stayed in a commercial guest house very near to the station. I travelled around quite a lot, having interviews, but I was getting despondent. I began to believe that my disability was standing in my way. I got into conversation with an insurance representative at the guest house and he told me of vacancies in Gloucester, Cheltenham and Worcester for insurance agents. Margaret, in the meantime, was looking in the nursing magazine for vacancies in hospitals other than those in Hertfordshire and the Home Counties.

I had arranged to keep in touch with the insurance representative and I returned to Watford. There was a telegram waiting for me from Mother asking me to come home at once because Father was failing fast. I phoned the factory and I got compassionate time off and within the hour, I was on my way to London to catch the next train to Plymouth. I had already phoned Margaret who was at home and told her the news.

This was 25th February and I arrived home early in the evening. Mother was pleased to see me and after I had seen Father, I asked Mother why had she not sent for me earlier to help her. Luckily, Joyce and cousins Winnie and June had rallied round and given Mother a hand. Bruce arrived next day and Aunts Anne and Hilda arrived on the Saturday.

Ron was on his ship which left Gibraltar on Sunday morning, 28th February. He would not get to Plymouth until Wednesday 2nd March at the earliest. Father died on that Sunday evening before 8.00 p.m. and cousin Winnie helped the nurses to lay him out.

Ron arrived in Plymouth on Wednesday morning, but it was not until later that day that he was able to come home to see Mother. The funeral was arranged for Thursday, my birthday, but I made no remark about it. It was not until after the funeral that someone realised that it was my birthday and, had they remembered, the funeral would have been put back a day.

Bruce went home the next day to Billericay, and Aunts Anne and Hilda went home on the Saturday. I stayed on until Sunday lunch-time then I caught the afternoon train to London. I had arranged to meet Margaret on Paddington Station, because she was catching the overnight train to Penzance, then the boat to the Scilly Isles. She was spending a week's holiday there.

After Margaret's holiday in the Isles of Scilly, she got herself a position at Worcester Royal Infirmary as a staff nurse. She lived in the nurses' quarters and began to get to know her way around in Worcester in her time off. I was busy trying to get a job in Worcester as well so I was travelling to and from Worcester whenever I could. In the end, I got a job with the Refuge Insurance Company as an agent.

Mr. Walsh had developed a lump on his neck and he had to have exploratory surgery on it. He insisted on being told what the result was and, as everyone feared, it was cancer. He had a course of treatment and it seemed to go into remission, which we were all pleased to know. He himself had decided that he was going to make the most of his leisure.

When I left Watford after Easter, I stayed in a hotel for a while until I found a flat to live in. Margaret had moved to Ronkswood Hospital to work and lived in the nurses' quarters there. I was not too keen on my job but I stuck at it knowing I could get another job later on.

Meanwhile, we were both making up a list of guests for our wedding, and a list of presents which we had been asked for. My cousin Peter in Moretonhampstead owned a printing works, he printed the invitation cards and that was his wedding present to us. The next thing was to persuade Margaret's father to come home and give her away. Several people on her side of the family had written to him and in the end, he relented and he did come home.

Although Wally was my life-long friend, he declined my invitation to be my best man. He thought it best that a local person would be a better idea, so I asked Dr. John and he accepted, which I and my friends were pleased about.

Olive and my niece Janet were chosen to be bridesmaids and I was hoping that Ron would get home in time for the wedding, too. He was the navigation officer on the cable ship which was laying a cable out in the Atlantic Ocean.

Margaret's brother Hugh was to be a sidesman because he would know all his relations that would be there. I had Bruce for my side.

Mrs. Sharp wanted to meet Dr. John before the wedding so I took him to meet her on the eve of the wedding. When we left,

John remarked that he had never been asked so many personal questions from a stranger before. He drove us back to his house in Watford where I was staying with him and his mother until the great day.

August the 6th dawned and I was hoping that today would be a very happy and memorable one for Margaret and me and one that we would never forget. The wedding was to be at 12.00 noon, so John, his mother and I left for Radlett about 10.00 a.m.. I had arranged to meet all my relations and friends at a café where we greeted each other and had coffee. Mother, Joyce, Janet, Bruce, Celia, Alan, Stephen, Aunt Anne and Wally were waiting for us along with Hunter and Bettine, when we got there. My relations had travelled from Billericay where they were the guests of Bruce and Celia, except for Aunt Anne, who came from Hounslow. Wally had travelled up from Bath, Hunter and Bettine having driven from St. Albans. I had to get Joyce and Janet to Margaret's house so that Janet could change into her bridesmaid's dress. Mother, Bruce and family also went to the house.

Dr. John and I left them there to make our way to the church where we were met by Rev. Christopher Newton, who was to conduct the service.

Margaret had requested Jeremiah Clarke's "Trumpet Tune and Air" for her walk up the aisle on her father's arm, but due to a misunderstanding, the organist played the "Trumpet Voluntary". The hymns we chose were "Love divine all loves excelling" and "Now thank we all our God" and the "Wedding March" by Mendelssohn. Margaret's father later asked me what the vicar, Mr. Newton, had said in his talk to us after we were married, during the first hymn. I told him politely that it was between Margaret, the vicar and myself.

The reception was held in the local Red Lion Hotel and it was Margaret's Aunt Olive who gave the toast to the bride and groom and not her father. In my reply, I thanked everyone for coming by land, sea and air to be there, which was true. Ron could not make it, he was still in the Atlantic Ocean somewhere.

After Margaret had changed into her going-away outfit, we took our leave from everyone, we got into Dr. John's car and set off for London airport. Hunter and Bettine followed in their car, which we had already arranged. We had made plans in case one of the cars had been 'doctored' with empty cans and 'just married' notices. Take off time was 5.00 p.m. and we were going to Jersey for our honeymoon. I had always wanted to visit the Island, having heard so much about it from people that I knew in Plympton who went there every year for a holiday.

We flew by Eagle Airlines in a Dakota aircraft which was a converted wartime aircraft. The plane vibrated very much after takeoff but we only took an hour to fly to Jersey. On our arrival at the airport we had a taxi to take us to the north of the island to our hotel in Bouley Bay. After booking in, we had our evening meal; we noticed that several other couples had got married that same day.

We went for a stroll in the grounds and ended up looking over the sea from the cliff garden. It was then that I sat down and got emotional when I realised that what had happened that day, no one would ever put asunder. It had been the happiest day of my life. Quite honestly, I thought for many years that I would never get married and yet, here I was celebrating just that. It was also our first experience of flying.

During our week there we made the most of getting around the island and going to dances in the evenings. We also did a day trip to St. Malo and Dinard in France, where we had a two hour coach trip around the French countryside. In Dinard itself we saw the new dam for the hydro electric turbines in construction. This was the first such dam in the world to use the incoming and outgoing tides in this way, to generate electricity at the mouth of a river.

The day after this trip we went on a day coach trip around the Jersey island coast anti-clockwise, starting and ending in St. Hellier. On another day trip we went to Guernsey by sea and had a halfday coach trip there also. Here we saw the famous carnations and grapes which were sent all over the world. We were also able to see the wartime hospital built by slave labour during the German occupation. It is not until you see such things for yourself that you are able to realise the suffering experienced by the islanders and prisoners of war alike. The other notable place we saw was the little chapel, constructed out of sea shells, which took one man many years to build.

There was one side about Margaret that I noticed on this trip which was her love of the sea and going on boats, ships and ferries. The sea was a little rough on returning from Guernsey and although some passengers were seasick, we were not. I was on my own, sitting in the lounge reading a paper and when I went to look for Margaret, I found her up on the deck enjoying every minute of it.

On our return to England, we had to get the train from Paddington Station in London for our return to Worcester. Margaret's parents and sister Olive were at the Station to see us off. We got back to the flat later that day and we had a fish and chip supper from a shop nearby.

The landlord of the flat was not very flexible with his rules and we could only have a bath on Fridays. Margaret overcame this by using the hospital facilities in the nurses' quarters.

Dr. John, who had been my best man, came to see us one weekend and we told him we were thinking of buying our own house. We decided that the best thing to do was to buy a house as soon as possible, so we put our names down with several estate agents. It took us three months to find what we could afford and we moved into our own house in Livingstone Street two weeks before Christmas.

I was still being hounded by the insurance company local manager to increase my clients with more sales of insurance policies, but after being out all day collecting, I was too tired to go out in the evenings canvassing for new business.

Margaret told me early in December that she might be pregnant and we decided not to tell anyone until she was absolutely sure. She was on duty on Christmas Day at Ronkswood Hospital and I went there in the afternoon and went on the ward to see her. One of the patients had told her a few days before that he knew a family called Dunkley from Devon and was she married to one of them. Margaret took me to see him and yes, we did know each other. He had been the taxi driver several years before when Father hired the taxi for the day to take us on a round trip to Lydford Gorge, Moretonhampstead,

Bovey Tracey and Newton Abbot, on the August Bank Holiday.

At the start of January, I had a very bad cold which developed into 'flu and I was put on the sick list by my doctor. The temporary manager that I had would not believe I was sick and called at my house to see me. I did not get up and answer the door so I did not know who was there. Margaret went on duty very early that morning and had left me still in bed. On her return, I was still in bed and I decided to get up for an hour or so.

When I went back to work the following week the manager accused me of being in bed with my wife, this information he had gleaned from the next door neighbour, when he had called. At this I leaned over the desk, grabbed him by the lapels of his jacket and shook him and told him to apologise, and as far as I was concerned, he could keep his job. Before going into my own house I called next door to see the widow and I told her off for telling lies to my manager and to mind her own business.

Margaret was livid when I told her what had happened at the office and almost burst into tears. It was then that she confirmed that she was pregnant. I also told Margaret that I had been to see the widow nextdoor and put her in her place. I left the insurance company shortly after this and once again, I was out of a job.

About a month later I did get myself an office job at the Metal Box Co. in Perrywood, which was only a short cycle ride from home.

Margaret worked to within three months of the due birth, so we had a holiday in May and went to Edinburgh for a week. Olive was working in a hospital there and had found us a bed-and-breakfast to stay at. She had also booked us several coach trips.

The landlady that Olive had found for us had a collection of dolls from all nationalities, and a set of toy monkeys called a monkey band. All these toys and dolls were in glass-fronted cabinets which covered all the walls in the room. In the centre of the room stood a large glass topped table in which she displayed all the English and Scottish paper currencies. It must have taken her years to collect and she did find it difficult to get it insured. We had never seen such a large collection before nor since.

We passed the construction of the new suspension bridge which would open the following year which was being built parallel to the Forth Railway Bridge over the Firth of Forth. We travelled to Callander, Loch Ness and across the Trossachs in the week while we were there. In Callender, our last stop, we visited a long wide barn which was full of all the tartan cloth. Some were made into kilts, some were ties, sashes and hats. There was a chart with all the clans listed and you could find out your own clan. We just bought a tie with four different tartans on and a piece of tartan cloth for Margaret to make a skirt with. We also enjoyed evening meals at the hospital where Olive was an anaesthetist.

We sent postcards to various relations and also to my ex landlady, Mrs. Baker, her sister and Mr. Walsh.

Mr. Walsh had not been at all well since the start of the year, but he was always asking after us. Unfortunately, he died just before the card arrived from us. Because we were now living in Worcester, neither of us was able to go to his funeral a few days after we returned from Edinburgh.

Margaret continued with the ante-natal clinic and everything was going along fine. I had even enlisted the help of my boss, Bill Freeman, in helping me to order the pram. He made all the necessary phone calls and the pram arrived in good time. Margaret went to the maternity wing of Shrub Hill Hospital late on Monday August 7th and our first son, John, was born the next day on August 8th about noon. I was not able to visit Margaret and see our new baby until visiting time at 7.30 p.m.. It seemed an eternity for those hours to go by before I could see them. After eight days I was able to bring them home and Margaret's mother came and stayed a few days while Margaret recovered. She did all the housework and getting the meals while she was with us, which we were very grateful for.

We kept in touch with my Mother, writing to her whenever I could; Margaret did the same writing to her mother.

We had the idea of having John baptised by Rev. Christopher Newton, who had married us in Radlett. Because we had selected my brother, Bruce, Margaret's sister, Olive, and her Uncle Raymond to be Godparents, it would be easier to hold the service there. We contacted Mr. Newton and he was delighted with the suggestion; it only remained to fix a date. John was baptised on Sunday 15th October and I must have had some holidays due to me, because we did not return home to Worcester until the Tuesday.

On our return to Worcester we settled down to the normal routine of my going to work at the Metal Box factory while Margaret was bringing up John and seeing to his daily needs.

As Christmas approached we were deciding what to get for Christmas and Margaret said she would make a pudding and a cake. We spent Christmas with her mother at "Little Meadows" in Radlett, where her brother, Hugh, and Uncle Raymond had Christmas lunch and tea with us. We had to return the day after Boxing Day because I had to return to work. We did not celebrate New Year's Eve being on our own, other than to have a drink at midnight.

Chapter Fifteen

ANOTHER BABY,
ANOTHER HOME...

The New Year of 1962 began by being very cold and frosty throughout January and February.

Margaret's sister, Olive, went to Persia in January to work in the hospital in Shiraz and it would be nearly three years before we would see her again.

When I could, I dug the back garden over and I was told that rats sometimes came up from the nearby railway lines and nested under the garden shed on next door's garden. Whenever the nextdoor neighbour saw me she would remark that I would never grow anything in the garden. However, contrary to her belief, she was amazed that I did grow a certain amount of vegetables, runner beans and potatoes in the garden with a major degree of success. She had a very old spaniel dog that was always ill, eventually she had to have it put down.

In the middle of March, the Queen Mother visited Plymouth and Devonport and she opened the new suspension bridge across the River Tamar. It was built along the north side of Brunel's famous railway bridge which carried the trains into Cornwall.

In June we left to spend a week at Plympton with Mother and she took care of John while we went to see the new bridge over the River. We also went together to spend a day with my cousin, Winnie Moreton, and her husband, Joe. We spent a day with Ron and Joyce, who had invited us to lunch and tea. Janet was then still at school.

On the Thursday I had arranged to take Margaret and John by bus to Bovey Tracey, leaving the pram with Mother. We were going to visit Aunt Hilda and Uncle Charlie for the day. Aunt Susie's husband, 'Vester, was not pleased about this because he thought that we should stay in Plympton and spend the time with her. I pointed out to him that we had already spent the Sunday with them and Mother and besides that, the arrangement was made by me before leaving Worcester. It turned out that we did see them on the Thursday because they were still with Mother when we got back in the evening.

By this time Margaret had been pregnant for about two months, but again we said nothing for a while.

We returned to Worcester and as we were leaving, I said to Mother that with 'Vester's attitude, he had spoilt some of our holiday to a certain degree, and she agreed with me. Of course, everyone was delighted to see Margaret, John and myself. However, when I did write and tell Mother that we were expecting an addition to the family, she wrote back and said she was not surprised because she thought Margaret was pregnant when we stayed with her in June, we could not hide it from her.

We spent a few days in Radlett near the time of John's first birthday when I had a week's holiday. Margaret's mother's immediate reaction to another baby was not favourable. She thought it was too soon after John's arrival. I told Margaret that I was not happy about her mother passing such remarks. It was our decision to have more children and not hers.

We had been suffering from a very hard cold winter with hoar frost for quite a few days. Margaret was expecting a baby at any time and early in the morning of 4th December Andrew arrived in a hurry (and he has been in a hurry ever since!) When the doctor and nurses arrived they were all covered in frost and looked more like snowmen. Margaret's mother arrived a day later to look after her and John and Andrew and stayed for about two weeks.

During this time the weather got much colder and I kept the coal fires going in both rooms downstairs to try and keep us all warm and to get the daily washing dry. We had logs of wood to supplement the coal which was getting in short supply, due to the demand and getting it distributed from the coal mines. Eventually, the water pipes had frozen, so we could only get water from a standpipe in the road.

We did have a Christmas dinner and that was about all we could manage. I had put a few decorations up to try and make it feel more festive, but the weather was getting us all down.

We were now well into January 1963 and the weather had still not improved and we still had to collect buckets of water from the standpipe. Several times we filled up the bath with water in the week and boiled it before we could drink it. How Margaret managed to do this so soon after giving birth to Andrew, I will never know. I was at work during the day so I could only help in the evenings and at weekends.

After six weeks relief came one weekend when some workmen came and offered to thaw the pipes of all the houses in the street with an electric heater. It cost us 10/- each per house, and fortunately I was advised to turn all the taps on before the pipes were thawed. The water flowed at last and we did not turn the taps off until all the air had been removed from the pipes by the pressure of the water. The next door neighbour did not do as we did and, in consequence, she had burst pipes which flooded her house with water running down the flex of the lights.

This was to be the coldest winter on record which lasted all through January and February. At last, in March, the weather began to improve and get warmer with very nice spring days.

I was still having routine checks on my leg about once a year at the hospital, but my foot had been giving me pain at times which I tried to ignore. I had been getting problems with my second and third toes on my right foot. They had begun to bend the wrong way and it was painful for me to walk. I went into hospital and I had both toes straightened out with pins in them to keep them straight.

While I was in hospital I was given a stool to weave with coloured string which became a hobby with me in later years. I had already made two or three rugs with rug kits which was another hobby that I had taken up.

My foot was kept in plaster for six weeks and I was surprised when it was decided to remove the plaster on a visit to the out-patients clinic that I had to be taken home by ambulance because I had no sock and shoe with me. After my return home I went to the post office to get my sick pay which had arrived that morning in the post. As I left home, a woman a few doors down the street accused me of wasting National Health money, being brought home by ambulance when I was able to walk. I told this woman life is not always what one sees and to mind her own bloody business, and walked on. When I got back home, I told Margaret about my encounter with this woman and that some people don't know when to mind their own business.

Olive had settled down in her new surroundings in Persia and she was glad to be away from the bad weather.

I was getting on well with my office job, my only regret was that the salary was not too well paid, but I had to stick it out because I realised it was still more difficult for me to get other employment, being disabled.

By July we had saved enough money to spend a week in Radlett with Margaret's mother with John and Andrew. On Sundays we took to going for walks as much as possible in the spring and summer time. When out on these particular walks we would discuss the houses that we were passing and the advantages that some of them had, and making comparisons with our own house.

We had decided that we did not want to stay in our house with frozen pipes again should we get another severe winter. So during this time, we started to get interested in looking at other properties. We wanted to get a larger house with larger rooms if possible, and with better plumbing and less risk of freezing pipes Towards the end of the year we had not found a house that was suitable and it was becoming a strain on both of us, so much so, that we nearly gave up looking altogether.

During the past year I had taken up wine-making as a hobby and I made various flavours of wine, but the one I excelled at making was elderberry. At one stage, I bought a cider jar from an off-licence near us and I made some potato wine. On checking it one evening to siphon it from the lees, the bottom of the jar broke away and the fluid filled the bowl it was standing in. Of course, it was ruined and I had to clear up the mess carefully.

In my wardrobe I had suspended a marrow in a nylon stocking filled with brown sugar and the smell of yeast and marrow combined permeated the bedroom. Eventually, I did transfer it into a demi-john jar with an air lock and when it had been bottled for a year or more, it tasted rather good.

As Christmas approached, we did stop looking for another house and we decided to start again in the New Year.

We spent Christmas at Radlett again, Margaret having travelled down a few days ahead of me with John and Andrew. I was able to catch the afternoon train from Worcester on Christmas Eve and I arrived in Radlett about 7.00 p.m., just in time to see John and Andrew before they went to bed.

I had made some gooseberry wine the previous year with the fruit from the garden in Radlett. I took a bottle of this with me and it was quite potent. Margaret's mother liked it very much, so much so that she had a good afternoon nap on one particular afternoon.

Bruce had asked me to meet Alan in London to collect a Christmas present, and when I met him he passed over three bottles to me. When I got back to Radlett I unpacked the bottles to find that I had got a bottle of port, sherry and whisky.

We returned home to Worcester and we celebrated the Old Year out and the New Year in on our own with some of the contents of the bottle that Bruce had given me. The next morning I returned to work.

We began 1964 by looking at more houses in the area and we looked at several, but they were not what we wanted. By now, we were getting tired of looking and if we did not find what we wanted, we were going to postpone looking for six months to see whether more and better houses came on the market.

Then, one day after I came home from work, Margaret said that she had passed a house that was up for sale in Fort Royal Hill. We went to the estate agent for the details and, after reading them through, we decided that there was no harm in looking at one more property. I went to see the property on my own first of all, and then I discussed what I had seen with Margaret. After this initial visit Margaret went on her own and later, we both went along, taking John and Andrew with us.

Margaret had certain misgivings about the house but I said that they could be overcome, given time.

After seeing the house in Fort Royal Hill, we weighed up the points in its favour and against. In its favour, was that it was much closer to get to the city for shopping (only ten minutes or less walking) and the nearest school was just a ten minute walk, as was the ante-natal clinic. There was a conservatory and a downstairs toilet and the kitchen was about nine feet square, which was double the size of the one in our present house. Both the dining room and the lounge were approximately twelve feet square, with two further feet into the bay window. Upstairs were three bedrooms and a bathroom and the back bedroom had a view of Fort Royal Park beyond which the Cathedral could be seen. It had only one bad point that we could see, which was the stairs being steep with narrow treads. The garden at the rear was twenty-odd feet wide and nearly three times as long, quite small really compared to the size of the house. On reflection, I think if we'd had a proper survey done, we would not have bought the house as it stood.

However, we did buy it and sold our own house in Livingstone Street. We moved in on September 21st, Margaret's mother having arrived three days before to help us to pack and move in. On our arrival, our new next-door neighbour greeted us with a large basket of apples from her tree and said that she was aged forty-eight years the wrong way round.

I had taken a week's holiday from work to get us moved and settled in. My immediate boss, who lived further down the Hill, called on me to ask me to return to work after only having had two days off. I was promised the other three days at a later date.

On the first day that we moved in we had delivered a second-hand dining room suite and a mahogany sideboard. Mrs. Sharp fell in love with the sideboard rightaway and polished it before filling it with the items Margaret wanted stored in it, such as the china, cutlery and the table cloths and mats. We also had our first fridge delivered and we found it a great help in keeping food and milk cool and fresh.

Our first weekend saw Margaret's mother return home to Radlett and we began to get ourselves organised and make the house our home. After we had been in the house a few weeks, the first thing we noticed that was wrong was that the wiring on the electrical circuits was not up to a safe standard. In the details from the estate agent it had stated that the house had been rewired, this was not true because the only things which had been replaced were the light and power switches. On a more detailed inspection, an electrician found that the cables were very old lead-covered ones with cracks in places, and that the junction boxes were made of tin, a real fire hazard in our estimation.

I managed to arrange with the electrician to rewire the house and while this was being carried out, Margaret took John and Andrew to Radlett for a week. I was able to get all the necessary materials from the factory at a discount, which saved us quite a lot of money had we got it from an outside electrical shop. Earlier in the year we had decided to save a certain amount of money each week towards the cost of Christmas, so that it would spread the costs of everything. However, we had to put some towards the cost of the rewiring this year.

Margaret returned with John and Andrew in time for her birthday, which was November 4th, after which we began to get ready for Christmas, to buy presents. Margaret made a cake and Christmas pudding and other Christmas items were bought to celebrate the festive season. This was celebrated by getting a large free-range chicken and not any of it was wasted. Margaret was very good at making other meals from it and also soup, which always went down well with John and Andrew during the cold weather. I also liked to get a piece of bacon to boil and eat it cold to supplement the chicken. My past experience of cooking large hams when as a shop assistant and manager came in very useful for this and Margaret used to leave it to me in buying it and to see to the cooking of it.

During January 1965, there was an outbreak of influenza and we were all smitten down with it. At one time we were all huddled together around the fire in the lounge. We dared not go out in the cold weather because we did not want to get any worse. A neighbour opposite offered to get the shopping which we were very grateful for.

When we had fully recovered, it was time for me to visit the hospital for another check on my foot and leg. Mr. Clark, the orthopædic consultant, discussed the possibility of operating on my foot to try and stop it from turning over onto its inside as it was beginning to do. This would be a series of bone grafts to be taken from my hip and placed into the bone in front of the ankle. I asked all manner of questions, because this was going to either improve my foot and the way that I walked or, at worst, a failed operation could mean that I would not walk very well, if at all. My leg would be in Plaster of Paris for at least six months and I'd not be able to go to work for that time.

I went home and discussed everything with Margaret and then with my employers the next day at the Metal Box Co.. They offered to keep me on their pay list on full pay for six months, while I was on the sick list, which was very good of them to make this offer.

Margaret and I knew from the financial side we would not have any worries, but she had misgivings about the success or otherwise of the operation. I told her that at work they had every confidence in Mr. Clark and that he had a good reputation as a consultant surgeon and that was one of the reasons why they'd offered to look after me. Three months later, after another examination by Mr. Clark, it was decided that he would go ahead and do the operation.

While all this was going on, we had a serious problem with the conservatory, in that the wooden bottom half was getting very flimsy from rotting and the weight of the glass roof and sides above could collapse at any time. I wrote to both Ron and Bruce to borrow the necessary £100 and Ron said that he could not help me. Bruce, on the other hand, said that if he'd had the money, he would have helped me out. This left me in a quandary because I did not know what to do next. I refused point blank to ask Margaret's parents or sister for help, because I did not think it right to do so.

Later on in the year, Bruce and Celia came to see us and saw the condition of the conservatory which was getting serious, so Bruce suggested I write to Aunt Anne for help. I had doubts about this because there had been a rumour in the past that

Father had asked for financial help but had never paid the money back. Mother was not in favour of this idea either, but the situation had got worse and I had no other option other than the bank or building society. So I wrote to Aunt Anne and I explained the situation to her; I had a cheque for £100 by return of post. I wrote back within a day or two and thanked her very much and promised to pay her back as and when I could, even if it was only £5 at a time.

I found a local builder who was prepared to rebuild the conservatory which, this time, would have a brick wall to put the glazed frames onto. We employed a bricklayer who built the walls very quickly, but the rest of the work took a very long time to get finished.

I went into hospital late in June, and the bone graft was taken from my hip and placed in the bone next to the ankle in three places. This was the most painful operation that I had ever experienced and I would never want another one like that again. I was given morphine and other drugs to ease the soreness and the pain, so it was two weeks or more before I was allowed to come home. I believe that had Margaret not been a nurse, I would have been kept in longer. With the sickness benefit plus my wages from work, we were able to save the extra money for future use such as more improvements to the house or towards a holiday, and in paying Aunt Anne back.

One Saturday morning after breakfast Margaret had left me in bed and John and Andrew downstairs to play while she went out shopping. She had not been gone very long before John called out that there was a man in the house. The man called out to me and it was the person who was doing my job while I was off work. He had brought all the paperwork with him and asked me to sort out a few problems. To me, this man was not capable of doing straightforward office paperwork. However, I sorted out what he wanted to know and I told him not to come here again with his problems and to leave them until I was back at work. I knew that he was only a temporary clerk, but he could also take my job away from me. I also knew that one of the department managers was related to him. All this time I was also chasing the builder to get the conservatory finished.

I had to visit the hospital every few weeks to make sure that the plaster did not crack or get too loose. This went on until a week before Christmas when the plaster was removed and then I had to have heat treatment and physiotherapy three times a week.

We celebrated Christmas and the New Year in the usual manner and soon I was able to return to work.

Chapter Sixteen

A CHANGE OF EMPLOYMENT

Early in the New Year of 1966 I returned to work and I was informed that the department managers had been reshuffled and that, therefore, I was now under a new manager. His attitude to me was totally different from what I had known prior to my operation. He was quite indifferent to me and, therefore, we did not see eye to eye on many things. His attitude was now that I was back at work, I had to give more than 100% to the work. He was also the one person who was related to the temporary clerk.

In certain areas the atmosphere was getting to be unpleasant in various offices where my work took me and, to a certain extent, with jealousy from one member of staff who was in charge of the "Kardex" system within the same office which we shared. I was so organised in my work and I was quick with it as well that at times I had time on my hands and I could relax on some days. This other member of staff was quite the opposite to me in his way of working, in that he was so disorganised in his approach to his work that he was always behind with it. He argued that I should help him and his team because I always seemed to be so organised. However, after a lot of discussions with the manager, he did get his way and I had to help out at times. When I did so, I noticed that he was relaxing and not pulling his weight. I complained to my boss about this man not pulling his weight and that my own work was getting behind, but all he did was to accuse me of being a trouble-maker. From then on there was a certain amount of animosity in the office.

As the summer approached, we had decided to have day trips

and we booked up with Midland Red Bus Company for four one-day trips. On the trip to Rhyl, it rained for most of the day and we seemed to have spent most of that time in the bus, not a very nice day at all.

The next trip was to Aberystwyth where it was a sunny day. Andrew asked why everyone was talking in a foreign language and we had to tell him that the local people were speaking in Welsh.

The third trip took us to Exmouth which was a very hot day. I bought a pair of swimming trunks from a local shop so that we could all go into the sea together. On our return journey the bus broke down in Malvern, the engine had seized up and we had to wait for another bus to get us back to Worcester. Because it was so late, we were dropped off near the bottom of the hill. As we walked up the hill, Andrew was amazed at how bright the moonlight was, it being about 1.00 a.m..

The last trip we did was to Barry Island in South Wales. We were not very impressed with that part of Wales and we were glad when it was time to leave for home.

We had also arranged to visit Bruce and Celia and my nephew Alan was to take us there by car, which he had hired for two days. On our arrival at Billericay the first thing that caught John and Andrew's eye was the TV set. Bruce switched it on and they were quite taken by it, so much so that they asked for it to be put on early in the day when there were no programmes on. When I was in the kitchen one day with Celia and Margaret, Celia told me to look through the serving hatch and observe John and Andrew. They were sitting down watching the TV and Celia remarked, "Isn't it about time you got yourself a TV set? Just look at them, absolutely glued to it." I said that I could not afford it yet.

At work, I had become very miserable and it upset my family to see me like this; on the strength of this I had begun to look for other employment. One of the staff in another office was a part-time telephonist at the G.P.O. telephone exchange, who said that there were a few vacancies there. I had an interview many years before in Plymouth for the same kind of work, but I did not pass the practical side of the interview. Had I done so, I would have started work in Truro. I applied for an application form which I filled in and in due course, I had an interview.

I was offered employment as a telephonist; the work would be evenings and at weekends, after the first six weeks' initial training Monday to Friday. I would be notified when I had to start. Meanwhile, in September, John began going to school now that he was five years old.

Towards the end of September I gave in my notice at the factory and the Personnel Department asked to see me. They wanted to know why, after nearly five years, I was leaving. I explained that the atmosphere had got very strained in the department where I worked and it was making me very unhappy. I was told that if I had told them of my position, they would have sorted it out and got me moved to another department, which they were still prepared to do.

I knew that I could almost double my wages at the G.P.O. after the first six weeks with only a little overtime. After giving it a lot of thought I turned down the offer from the factory. After I gave in my notice I was sent home from the factory with a high temperature by the nurse. I had got flu so I was off sick instead of working out my two weeks' notice.

I did my initial six weeks' training and, at first, I found it rather strange being at home all day until it was time to go to work just after 5.00 p.m. One of the trainees with me hailed from Plymouth and his accent was broader than mine. However, we got on well together and the next thing we found out was that the chief night supervisor had been an air-raid warden in Plymouth during the War. Our training supervisor was an ex-major from the Army and, at times, he could be awkward with us, and he had his favourites. I was not one of them and he used to pick on me quite a lot. We took our final exams and when he knew that we had all passed, he was a different person. His attitude changed and he took us all out for a drink to celebrate. When I got home later that evening, Margaret and the boys were overjoyed that I had passed; it meant that my wages would now begin to increase and that our financial situation would improve.

Margaret had helped me to learn the abbreviations that we used when taking calls which we needed to be perfect on or else the wrong subscriber might be charged for a phone call.

I began to save my money and each month, I was sending Aunt Anne some money because I did not want to be beholden to her, and I would have felt guilty had I not paid her back.

Margaret had also begun to work, nursing terminally ill patients at night for the Marie Curie Fund. This pay was not very good and I said that I could earn quite a lot more on an all night on overtime. This was the plum in the overtime which was allocated on a rota basis to be fair to all the telephonists.

Then the day staff supervisor began to ask me to work for them on overtime, so from the financial point of view, I had done the right thing by leaving the factory and working for the G.P.O.. Margaret then stopped working and concentrated on bringing up John and Andrew and looking after the house and garden.

I eventually paid off the money to Aunt Anne that I had borrowed, and she wrote and told me that anytime in the future that I needed to borrow money again, I was to ask her and she would willingly lend it to me. Of course, this was very good to know, but Margaret and I agreed that we would never borrow money again like that from anyone. In my formative working life, having to learn the hard way the value of money, we became very thrifty and started to build up our assets as much as possible for any repairs that we might need doing to the house.

What I did next was to invite Aunt Anne to come and stay with us, and she accepted our invitation.

After one storm we had to have slates replaced on the roof so I had to claim from the insurance company to pay for the damage. The roof, in a sense, became an obsession with me and over the next few years, I was always afraid that during every storm it would be damaged.

At the telephone exchange one rule agreed with the management and union was that if you worked on Christmas Day and not Boxing Day one year, the next year you had Christmas Day off and worked the Boxing Day; a record was kept for this. No one was allowed to take any annual leave during the festive and New Year season. However, some rules were not maintained and a reasonable Christmas atmosphere prevailed for a few days when we were on duty, but I much preferred being at home with my family.

Also, if you were unfortunate to be on duty when the clocks were put forward for Summer Time, you were expected to be on duty when the clocks were put back in the autumn. I was caught for this one year and I made sure that I was not going to fall for that again. I avoided it by asking for a week's leave which was granted the next year and I did not work those all night duty weekends again.

The conservatory was eventually completed and we were glad to see the end of the builder. His bad language to his son, who was working with him, was picked up by John and Andrew because they repeated the words to Margaret. This upset her a great deal because she was not used to hearing such language.

Life went on as normal and as we had had the one day trips, we still spent a few days in Radlett when I had a holiday.

At Christmas-time, Margaret's mother came, loaded with presents and a cake, and stayed for two days. She then had to return and get ready for Christmas at Radlett when her friends would be seeing her.

We spent a quiet time ourselves at that time, mainly because I was working and I refused to work any overtime so that I could be home as much as possible and to help Margaret with the preparations.

During the bad weather I was now walking to work and not risking to cycle; quite often I managed to get a lift home by car by other operators, so I was glad when the spring and lighter evenings came.

Aunt Anne was going to visit us in early summer 1967. She wanted to see for herself the rebuilt conservatory for which I had borrowed the money. When she arrived in the evening by coach it had taken all day to get here from London. When we met her we walked home from the coach stop in Croft Road and it took us nearly three parts of an hour. We were all tired, especially Aunt Anne when we arrived home. It never crossed my mind to order a taxi and Aunt Anne was annoyed that I did not think of it. However, we made her feel very welcome and as I was at work every evening, she spent most of the time with Margaret.

She was pleased to see the improvement to the conservatory and repeated the offer again of borrowing from her if I needed any help.

The one remark she did make was that the best investment was in bricks and mortar (i.e. a house).

We had arranged and booked a holiday in mid-June in Worthing for a week's holiday. Mother was to join us there after staying with Bruce and Celia, who were to drive her to Surrey where Henry Goodman, a long-standing family friend, would drive Mother to Worthing from his house. We all met on the sea front in Worthing and we took Mother to the guest house we had booked. We had been allocated two very small rooms at the top of an annexe house several houses away from the guest house. We had to share a bathroom with another young couple who seemed to commandeer it each time we needed to use it.

We spent the evening in the lounge where everyone except us were afraid to speak or move. Eventually, I put the TV on for John and Andrew to watch, and we got moaned at by the other guests. We stuck it out until coffee was served, then we left for the annexe. The couple there had the radio on very loud and we asked them to turn the volume down. This was refused so not one of us had very much sleep that night.

Next morning we went for our breakfast, which was very cold, consisting of a fried egg, bacon and bread, which none of us could finish. When the owner came to clear away the dishes we complained about the couple's noise all night long and about the food being cold, but her attitude was that she wasn't bothered.

We then had a quick discussion between us and decided to cut our losses and move out. I stayed with Mother and John, and Andrew went with Margaret to find another guest house. Within an hour they came back to say that they had found a more suitable place. We had already packed our clothes etc. ready for the move and, by 11.00 a.m., we had booked in at an hotel further along the front. We were made to feel welcome straightaway, so we quickly settled in and then left to explore the town.

We had booked to go to Arundel Castle on the Tuesday, but John was not feeling well, so I took him to see a doctor who said that he had got glandular fever and suggested that, on our return home, I was to take him to see our own G.P.. For most of that day, John and I stayed in our hotel, but I did take him with me to get his prescription. We all returned home by train, via London, where Bruce met us to take Mother to Paddington for the train to Plymouth.

I went to see Mother again in Plympton and while I was there, I went to see my cousin, Winnie, one evening; at that time her son, Christopher, was home from university.

There was a crisis with finances within the Government and the Prime Minister, Harold Wilson, had introduced an emergency budget. Purchase Tax was to be increased in the following September on such things as luxury items which included TV sets. In the same news it mentioned an item about convicts in prison would have their TV viewing reduced. On hearing this, I remarked, "Here am I, I have never been convicted of a crime and married with two children and I cannot afford a TV, and yet there are convicts in prison who have that luxury."

When I returned home to Worcester, I discussed this with Margaret and we decided that if convicts could have TV for leisure, so could we. We rented a TV set from then on and our first one was a black and white set. Colour TVs were much more expensive at that time, but at least we had got a set to watch. For a while, TV took over from other things, such as the radio and records, but eventually we were able to compromise once the novelty of the TV had worn off.

In September, we had to call the doctor in because both John and Andrew had got tonsillitis. It was decided that both needed to have their tonsils removed because they kept getting very bad colds, and now tonsillitis and glandular fever.

Mother had also not been very well and it was decided that she should live with one of us. Ron and Joyce could not have her, and we had no room here with only three bedrooms, so it was decided, after a lot of discussion, that she would live with Bruce and Celia for a few months.

It was arranged that Margaret would go to Plympton on her own and stay with Mother to help her in sorting out her belongings. Ron and Joyce organised getting Mother's furniture into a sale. Margaret returned home to Worcester and Ron helped Mother get to the station. Bruce met her at Paddington Station and took her to Billericay.

Andrew started school in September, so both boys were now at school, which gave Margaret more time to herself. Each day she had to take John and Andrew to school; sometimes I would meet them at lunchtime and take them back again.

Having TV put a different aspect on the celebrations for Christmas and the New Year. We were now able to watch all kinds of entertainment. Margaret liked to watch the morning service and the Queen's speech during the day, when for a while she could have a break after cooking the dinner.

Early in 1968 we booked up for a week's holiday in Weston-super-Mare for the following July, when John and Andrew would be on holiday from school. This gave us something to look forward to and we were saving as much as we could which, at times, was quite difficult to keep to. However, the great day arrived and off to the station we went to catch our train, which took us there without having to change trains. We arrived in the late afternoon and we got to the hotel by taxi. After we booked in we decided to go for a walk and to see what the resort had to offer us in the way of entertainment and, of course, the bathing.

After our first meal at the hotel, we went out again to see the lights and walk along the front.

Next morning, we went onto the pier where there was an amusement arcade with plenty of penny machines to play. In half-an-hour the four of us had spent £3. When I realised this, I pointed out that spending money in such a way it would not last us the week because there were a number of other things we wanted to do and go on some trips etc.. We did not use the machines again for the rest of the week.

My friend, Wally, and his wife, Daphne, drove from Bath to see us while we were there, it being quite a long time since we had seen each other. For the rest of our stay we enjoyed ourselves so much that we decided to return again the following year.

We had a rough journey back to Worcester. The train was packed to capacity, but eventually we arrived home safe and sound.

The next thing to do was jam-making with the summer fruits. This was followed by making chutney. I pickled some onions and then some eggs in the hope that it would all be ready to eat at Christmas. After this, Margaret made the Christmas puddings and a cake, so it was a busy autumn for us.

At the end of November, Margaret paid a visit to Chippenham to see her mother and to take the presents for Christmas with her. On her return in the evening we met her at the station and she was loaded with Christmas gifts from her mother.

We had our usual Christmas and New Year celebrations and John and Andrew had school and other parties to go to, which, on the whole, they enjoyed.

We booked up our next holiday at the same hotel in Weston-super-Mare and sent off the deposit, but this time Margaret's mother was coming as well, and she would drive her car from Chippenham to Weston.

After having my name down for an allotment I was at last allowed to rent one from the council. It was in Stanley Road, almost next to the school. We began to prepare the ground to grow our own vegetables, in the hope that we could save money in buying them. It was hard going from the start, digging the ground over. I was not as strong as some men are when it came to the digging etc., so Margaret began to help with that work.

I managed to get two varieties of potatoes planted and we had a good return, but we were well stocked for the greens that I grew such as peas, runner beans, cabbages and leeks, plus radish, lettuce and beetroot.

Margaret suggested getting some raspberry canes and as she knew from her mother's garden how to grow them, we ordered them from a nursery. From then on each June we had a lovely crop with which Margaret was able to make jam. This kept us busy at weekends and in the evenings and the time was drawing near for our next holiday to Weston.

We had an offer of a lift from one of the men at work who said he was going near to Weston and that he could fit us all in his car. We arranged that he would pick us up early on Saturday morning, but it was 11.30 a.m. before we left Worcester. It was quite a tight fit to get two adults and two children into the back seat of the car, which was not very comfortable for us.

Instead of going straight down to Weston he decided to go via Chepstow and on towards Cardiff before crossing over the new suspension bridge, so it was nearer teatime before we got to the hotel where Margaret's mother had been since lunchtime waiting for us. We were very annoyed with this man for such a bad trip in more ways than one. Margaret had arranged to meet her mother by lunchtime and the boys were very restless long before we got to the hotel. All in all, it was a bad start to the holiday.

We spent the first day on the beach and, in the evening, Margaret and I left the boys with her mother and we went to the theatre to see a play. During the rest of the week we went to Wookey Hole and then on to Cheddar Caves and climbed Jacob's Ladder. We also went to see Wells Cathedral on another day. We quite liked the Cathedral and its construction, with the supports for the roof and tower. However, I do not think the boys were very interested in the building at the time.

Mrs. Sharp took us in her car for these trips, which we all enjoyed. The rest of the week we stayed in Weston itself. We had booked the same hotel that we had the previous year, but we noticed we did not receive the attention as before. The owner and staff made us welcome at first, but their attitude was not so good as the previous year. From this experience we decided never to book the same hotel if we intended to return to the same resort in future years.

After our experience with the car going on holiday, I was glad that we had booked to come home by train. Margaret's mother drove us to Bristol to catch our train back to Worcester which was better than from Weston.

On our return it was back to work for me and in the evenings and at weekends, we went to the allotment to gather more produce. As the autumn approached, we reduced the time that we spent on the allotment, but we dug it over ready for next year.

Bruce and Celia were in the midst of selling their bungalow for a four-bedroom house in another part of Billericay, so in October Mother came to stay with us until they had completed the move.

Soon after her arrival Mother had a letter from a solicitor in Torquay which had a cheque for £500 in it. This was money that had been left to her by Aunt Nell, who had died the year before.

At this time I was suffering from a bout of haemorrhoids, which gradually got worse. Towards the end of October they burst while I was at work and I was sent home early. Next morning, I went to see the doctor. He referred me to a specialist at the hospital and I had to stay at home resting until I was sent for. I waited three weeks and I was admitted during the last week of November. Margaret was able to visit me most days on her own, leaving Mother here looking after John and Andrew when they returned from school.

On the Sunday they all came to see me and Andrew wanted to know if I would be home for his birthday. I said that I did not know, but I would try to be well enough to be home in time. As it turned out, I was allowed home the day before his birthday on December 4th. When he came home from school I heard him ask Margaret if I would be home for his birthday. She said she was not quite sure. He then asked, "Where is Grandma?" and Margaret said she was in the lounge. When he opened the door the first person he saw was Grandma; then he saw me. The expression on his face said it all. He was pleased as punch to see me and that I was home in time for his birthday.

Mother stayed with us for Christmas and New Year because Bruce and Celia had been delayed with the move to the new house.

Chapter Seventeen

A LIFE GIVEN
& A LIFE TAKEN

I did not return to work until early in the New Year. Work had ceased on the allotment well before Christmas and we were busy looking after Mother, as well as getting organised for the festive season.

Bruce arrived in the middle of January 1970 and stayed overnight in a hotel nearby for bed and breakfast. The next day he took Mother back to Billericay. In some respects, we were all sorry to see her leave us, but in others it meant that we could return to normal and get on with our lives.

As spring approached we were planning what to grow the next season besides potatoes and greens.

Overtime became more plentiful again so John and Andrew did not see very much of me because I was at work most evenings and at weekends.

Because we were growing a lot of vegetables and fruit, we decided to buy a freezer to store the food in so that we could use it in the winter. Our first one was small because we had to keep it in the conservatory as there was no room in the kitchen for it.

In the early summer Ron and Joyce came to see us and while the boys were at school, Ron drove us to Stratford-on-Avon where they treated us to lunch. We got back before school ended, so Ron went and picked the boys up from school in his car and took them for a ride before tea. For once, I had an evening off so I did not have to leave for work after tea was over.

As the year progressed, we began to decorate the bedrooms and to afford this, we did not go away for a holiday. John and Andrew helped us with the preparations, stripping the paper off the walls, which both of them enjoyed doing. After two bedrooms had been completed, we still had the allotment to see to so it was a very busy time that summer.

As the autumn approached, we went looking at wallpaper for our front bedroom. Then I had to go into hospital for yet another operation on my foot. When it was decided to do our bedroom I had been sent home from hospital so I was in bed recovering. I had had my ankle bones reset, so Margaret and John did the redecorating together while I lay in bed.

By this time, Margaret had been pregnant for five months and the baby was expected to be born in late-April next year.

At work, there were problems between the G.P.O. management and our trades union over a pay award which also involved the postmen. There was talk of a strike being taken which was the last thing that I wanted with an addition expected in the family.

We got through Christmas but I had to work part of the holiday. At least I was at home during the day when John and Andrew were home from school.

In January 1971, we all came out on strike which included the postal workers and the telephonists, it being a national strike. This lasted for nine weeks. We existed on subsistence allowance and the money that we got depended on our own individual circumstances. It was very hard at times to make ends meet during the strike, but we struggled on the best we could and I was wishing for it to end sooner rather than later.

This was also the same time that we were going to be converted to decimal currency instead of staying with pounds, shillings and pence. In my view, it was a very great mistake, knowing full well that the cost of living would more than double overnight, which proved to be correct. For instance, prior to decimal day we had 240 pence in the £ but that would reduce to 100 pence. Vegetables such as carrots, onions and potatoes were 3, 4 and 6 old pence per pound, the next day, 15th February, they were priced at 4, 5 and 6 new pence a pound, so therefore, 3 new pence became equal to 7 old pence, 4 new pence became equal to 9 old pence, and 6 new pence became equal to 1/3d old money. The shops denied putting the prices up but I have always maintained that the country had been taken to the cleaners by the government of the day and that it cost this country billions of pounds. The Australian Government had warned our government not to make 100 pence to the £ because, from their experience, when they converted to dollars they had lost billions in their conversion; but the English government would not listen and ignored their advice.

The strike duly ended in mid-March so we were all back to normal working within hours. There was an anticlimax to all this with a little bit of bad feeling between those who'd supported the strike and those who'd broken it. In the end, it was to no avail because, at the end of the year, we got the increase that we had struck for and we all lost nine weeks' salary.

The next thing that I had to arrange was to get a week's leave to coincide with the week that the new baby was due. Margaret's sister Olive was going to come to look after Margaret and John and Andrew prior to the new baby's arrival. I managed to get a week off from 24th April and Olive arrived on that day also.

We all went out to the cinema to see "Paint Your Wagon" on the Monday evening and we enjoyed the film immensely. Two days later, as forecast for that week by Margaret, the new baby arrived on the 28th, and she had another baby boy. He arrived just after 8.00 a.m. so John and Andrew were able to see him before they went to school.

Olive stayed until the Saturday, 1st May, when Ron and Joyce arrived with Joyce's sister, Thelma. They had come because Joyce was to stay for a week to look after us all. Ron and Thelma went back to Bath later that day.

The new baby was to be called Kenneth Norman and in the first week of July, he was Christened by Margaret's father at St. Peter's Church, which was to be the last Christening before the Church was closed for ever. My niece, Janet, was his godmother and my friend, Wally, was godfather along with

Hunter, my other friend from St. Albans in Hertfordshire.

When Kenneth was two months old we had a visit from Bruce and Celia, who brought our cousin Doris to see us. She was here on a holiday from Australia, being the eldest daughter of Uncle Harold, Mother's brother.

At work, we were all trying to get as much overtime as possible to make up for the loss of wages that the nine weeks' strike had caused us. This caused some bad feeling when some staff managed to get more than their fair share of the overtime.

Kenneth began to thrive and put on weight and he was growing very fast.

We later had a visit from Hunter and Bettine with their children who were camping in the Vale of Evesham for a week's holiday. They only came for the day, but it was good to see them all once again.

The rest of the year was normal, looking after the house, garden and the allotment, so there was plenty to do.

I had ordered another rug kit to make in the winter and now I had a rack to hold the canvas while I put the stitches in. This was a great help until reaching the last few rows, when it was not possible to use the rack on the double thickness of canvas.

This was Kenneth's first Christmas and we all did our bit to make it a good one for him. By then, he was eight months old and able to sit up and take notice of what was going on. We had to stop Andrew from taking food from his Mum's plate, which he had been doing for quite some time. The only answer was to give him a larger helping, but then Margaret had a smaller helping of the meal.

Both John and Andrew had been having swimming lessons, but John was not at all keen on this, and in 1972 he was due to go to the secondary modern school. This was a concern to Margaret and myself because we wanted the best for him, so we went to see his form teacher and headmaster. We were advised that the one school was too large in pupil numbers so it was suggested that we apply for a place for him at the Bishop Perowne school which was supported by the Church of England.

At the end of the school year in July, I took John to see the school, which was two miles from home. After that there was

173

an introductory evening for new pupils and parents. We were introduced to all the teaching staff and some of them used to be on the staff at John's old school. He settled in quite well and, at first, he travelled by bus, but he decided it was quicker to walk home than wait for a bus, and he kept it up until he left school five years later. He had homework to do and this had to be done before he could watch the television or go out to play.

While this was going on my work kept me busy and I was getting quite a lot of day overtime besides my normal evening and weekend duties.

On the allotment we had a very good row of raspberry canes which gave us a very good crop most summers. Margaret's mother had some in her garden, so before we knew each other, Margaret's mother had taught her how to look after the canes to get the best results. This was passed on to me by Margaret and from then on, we always enjoyed them. Margaret would make jam with some of the fruit and some we would freeze.

Kenneth became very ill with a fever but the doctors could not find the real cause for this. We thought a change of air might do him good so we arranged to go to Calne and stay with Olive for a few days. The doctor was not too keen on the idea at first, but Margaret said that Olive was in practice there as a doctor and that she would get a doctor from the practice to examine Kenneth should he not improve.

We went to Calne by taxi with Margaret nursing Kenneth most of the way. On our arrival, Olive had Kenneth examined and they gave him an injection and he slept for almost twenty-four hours. There is a park opposite Olive's bungalow, so I took John and Andrew there to play, or we went further away for walks. As Wally and Daphne lived in Bath, they came to Calne to see us while we were there and it was the first time for them to see Kenneth.

Kenneth began to improve after his long sleep and he was much better by the time we had to return home. After we came home John and Andrew went back to school and I returned to work. Margaret took Kenneth for a check-up with the doctor and he was pleased to see that he was so much better. We never did find out what was really wrong with him.

During the beginning of September we had news that my brother Frank was ill, but we were not sure of the form of his illness. Mother, who was still living with Bruce and Celia in Billericay, kept us all informed when she got any news from Rhodesia.

In October I had taken a few days leave to coincide with the school half-term, and one night about 10.15 p.m., we heard the front door bell ring. It was a telephonist, asking me to phone Bruce because he had some bad news. I went to the public callbox and a supervisor at the exchange connected me with Bruce. The news was that Frank had died of leukaemia on the 25th October.

Although none of us had seen him since he left England in 1953, it was still a shock to try and realise that he had died.

Up to this point we did not have a phone, so, to avoid having problems in getting news to us in the future, I applied for a phone. After waiting a month, we had our first phone fitted and connected; this was going to be a boon to me in respect of overtime working. Both the day and night clerical staff officers were phoning me to help out on overtime. This boosted my income a great deal. It also meant that we could be contacted by relations on both sides of the family.

We had decided to have a seaside holiday for 1973, in Weymouth, so after getting the brochure, we booked up a guest house on the sea front. We booked up to travel by coach rather than have two or three changes by rail. It took almost all day to get to Weymouth and the coach park was situated on the outskirts of the town. This meant that there was only a taxi service into Weymouth, so, after travelling all day we then had to queue up for a taxi. It was almost an hour before we got to the guest house and booked ourselves in. The one drawback was the sharing of the toilet and bathroom facilities in the guest house, which did not suit us at all.

As we were close to Portland, it was easy for Janet and Les to spend some time with us. They went to Portland to live because Les was a draughtsman there for the Admiralty. Janet, being a qualified librarian, worked in the prison library there.

We had a fairly good week in Weymouth and on the Friday,

we booked a taxi on the sea front to take us to the coach park on the Saturday morning for our return journey back to Worcester. The taxi let us down by not turning up and one of the guest house staff managed to get us a taxi which got us to the coach park just in time to board the coach. It took us all day to get home and I vowed that we would never rely on taxis ever again.

I also decided that, on future holidays, I wanted en-suite facilities, nothing else would do. If they were not available, I refused to book that hotel or guest house.

After our return we had the new term to look forward to for John and Andrew and then on to Christmas.

Assuming there was no more that could be done to improve my foot, I had stopped going to see the orthopaedic surgeon unless anything else went wrong with it. There was only one bone graft holding in place now because one had not fused at the time of the operation, and the other had collapsed. I was still able to get new footwear every year and having my shoes repaired on the N.H.S..

Over the years Wally and I kept in touch by letters to each other, but at one stage Daphne wrote to say that Wally was not very well and had been in hospital. I arranged to visit them when I had a day off from work and I went to Bath. Daphne met me at the station with the car and drove me to their house. Wally did not look very well and he was very slow when he walked. I could remember when he was a very fit man, being in a hockey team for the Civil Service.

After I returned home I told Margaret that I did not like seeing Wally looking so ill. He had got cancer of the lungs from asbestos poisoning from his days working in Devonport dockyard.

Christmas and the New Year were celebrated in the usual manner and I phoned Wally to find out how he was. Daphne answered the phone and the news was not very good at all. Wally was at home but only for Christmas Day and Boxing Day, then he would have to return to hospital for more treatment.

* * * *

During the early days of January 1974 I was at work when Margaret had a phone call from Daphne to say that Wally had died. When I arrived home I rang Daphne straightaway and offered my condolences. I was upset that I was not able to go to his funeral. After that, Daphne has kept in touch with me over the years, mainly because Wally and I were such good friends and because he was Kenneth's godfather.

Mother had been living with Bruce and Celia for a few years and she came to stay with us each summer for a month or six weeks so that Bruce and Celia could have a holiday and a break from looking after her. However, this year, it was decided that as Mother was getting more frail as she got older, it would be better for all concerned if she went into an old people's home where she would have more attention. She eventually moved into such a home in Laindon in Essex, and it was not too far for Bruce to visit her. I went to see her as and when I could, which was not often because of the distance I had to travel.

Andrew was now eleven years old but he had to wait until September before he could join John at Bishop Perowne School.

I was still smoking in spite of being warned by the doctor the previous November to give it up. In May, I work up early in the morning with a very bad attack of coughing. Margaret remarked, "About time too! You have already woken up the rest of the family." I said, "Well, if that's what smoking does to me, I will stop from now on." I did just that and I have never had a cigarette since that time. For a while, I ate sweets but I soon gave that up.

During the summer months, Mrs. Sharp, Olive and Betty (Olive's friend) would come to see us, usually on a Sunday, and they would stay for lunch and tea. At other times, only Olive and Betty came and we would then go out to lunch and drive to either Herefordshire or Shropshire and then park the car and go for a walk before returning home.

Margaret enjoyed these visits to the full because looking after an all male family, she was glad of a change with Olive and Betty to talk to. Their next visit coincided with Andrew's birthday early in December, when we were treated to lunch by Olive to celebrate and, as usual, the exchange of Christmas presents was carried out. I had an adjusted duty which, to me, was not very good. I seemed to be more at work than at home for the festivities.

1975 dawned with news that Alan and Pam were going to be parents in July and that also Janet and Les were expecting their first baby at the same time. First to arrive safe and sound was Claire to Janet on the 11th of July. Then on 19th July, a son was born to Pam and was to be called Lee. So now both Ron and Joyce, Bruce and Celia were grandparents and I became a great uncle. Alan and Pam went for a holiday in France later that summer, but I think Janet and Les paid visits to their respective parents.

We had a visit from Olive and Betty for Andrew's birthday when they brought the Christmas gifts for us and they went back with the gifts from us.

Betty was a supervisor at the Swindon telephone exchange and she mentioned that the G.P.O. were talking in terms of reduced staffing levels, which meant that there would most likely be redundancies. This was of great concern to Margaret and me because it was possible that I could be made redundant.

We spent the Christmas and New Year on our own and because of the holidays, I had adjusted duties for the two weeks.

It turned out not to be a very happy time for Bruce and Celia. Mr. Bowdler, Celia's father, died on Boxing Day.

Because of my adjusted duties I had several days off together and I did not have to return to work until Friday January 1st 1976.

That day, a terrible storm had erupted over the whole country. Some areas were devastated with storm damage and it was very frightening. I had to report for work at 11.00 p.m. and had an adjusted night duty until 8.00 a.m. January 2nd. Walking to work I saw slates being blown off the roofs of the houses and other structural damage was being done and when I got to work, I was shaking all over from the severity of the storm. I phoned Margaret to make sure that she and the boys were all right and to let her know that I had managed to get to work without mishap.

We were very busy all night with emergency calls and I was glad when the storm began to abate at about 3.00 a.m.. Between

6.00 and 7.00 a.m. the next morning I had a premonition that something was wrong somewhere, but what it was I did not know. When I got home, I still did not feel right and I told Margaret how I was feeling. She tried to reassure me that we were all all right and the house did not have too much damage, but I insisted that it was something else that was wrong somewhere. She then encouraged me to get some sleep and that she would wake me about 4.00 p.m. in time for me to return to work by 6.00 p.m..

The weather reports were very bad with many accidents and people injured or killed all over the country and trees uprooted and blown down with millions of pounds worth of damage to properties, etc.. Margaret brought me a cup of tea at 4.00 p.m. as promised and she said that she had got some bad news for me. Bruce had phoned to say that Alan had been in an accident with his car that morning going to work. I asked her how badly was he injured and Margaret replied, "It's worse than that; he is dead. He was killed in his car." I then asked, "What time did this happen?" and Margaret said, "Between six and seven this morning." I then remembered the premonition that I had had at that precise time. I lay in bed in disbelief. I could not take it in; I could not believe what I had heard, nor the premonition.

At work that evening I was given permission to phone Bruce and Ron and we had a three-way conversation. Stephen had to identify Alan because Bruce was caring for Celia and he had to go and tell Mother.

I was like a zombie for the next week, feeling in a daze and not knowing what to do. I could not bring myself to go to Alan's funeral service, which was less than a week after his grandfather was buried. Bruce and Celia were devastated and it was going to take a very long time for them to recover from this.

This left Pam to bring up Lee on her own, which she did very well. She went to live with Bruce and Celia later that year after Alan's estate had been settled. A few months before this happened, Bruce had applied for a transfer from Southend-on-Sea and he was transferred to Poole, Bournemouth.

They bought a house in Corfe Mullen in Dorset and had Alan's ashes interred there in the cemetery. The house had four bedrooms so now they could put friends and relations up when they wanted to.

Pam managed to get a part-time job to help in bringing Lee up, but overall it was not a happy time for any of us for several months.

Betty's remarks about the G.P.O. turned out to be true so I had this worry over me, not knowing if and when the redundancies would start and whether or not it would involve my position. Towards Christmas we were told officially that, next year, redundancies would begin from the end of March, not a very nice prospect for the new year.

Chapter Eighteen

IN WORK & OUT OF WORK

I think many in the family were now hoping for a better year after the previous one.

With the threat of losing my job, financially for us things were not going too well. We had more maintenance to be done on the house and this was a drain on our resources.

We had booked a holiday at Lyme Regis and then we cancelled it, and I wrote and told Bruce and Celia that we had done so. He then invited us to stay with him at no charge if we could see our way clear to pay the fares to get there. The only way we could do this was to travel by coach and that is what we did.

During our stay we went into Poole nearly every day and Bruce also took us for walks around Corfe Mullen and we did visit the cemetery to see Alan's headstone.

When we returned home I heard some bad news from work. While I had been away the chief supervisor and three assistant supervisors had been made redundant, plus another four telephonists, and they were shortly going to leave. The G.P.O. had decided that more redundancies were to take place to reduce the staffing levels even further and to increase the number of all-night duties. Because I was fifty years old, I was told that I could apply to be made redundant or I would be expected to increase my workload if I stayed on. I applied for a day position but I was informed that there were no vacancies at that time.

Actually, it was their polite way of telling me that my services were no longer required, in spite of my registered disabled card (thank you so much for a caring employer).

I had recently seen my doctor who said that I looked rundown and that I was working far too many hours. He then asked about the future, so I told him about the two all-night duties that could be done on consecutive nights. His advice to me was on health grounds not to do that and that I should think seriously about the redundancy offered. I talked it over with Margaret and the boys and they said they would be glad to have me at home in the evenings.

John left school in July and was due to go to the Worcester Technical College in September for further education for a year. In September I left the G.P.O. as a telephonist with a pension that began on September 17th, but it was frozen to one figure for five years. I was now unemployed again after being in work for more than twenty years since the last time.

John began his new course at the time that I left the G.P.O. and by all accounts, he was coping with it all right.

The news from Mother was not too good; she had not been feeling well. Our cousin Julie went to see here as also did Ron, Joyce and Janet. Bruce also went to see her but I did not, thinking that I would visit her much later when I hoped that she would be better and she seemed to be improving.

I was still writing to her nearly every week and she would answer them, but I did not mention the problems at work to her. I knew it would worry her, but I noticed that her handwriting was not as good as it had been. She made the excuse that her eyes were not too good.

However, when it got to December, Mother stopped writing and she began to get worse, but we were assured by the staff looking after her that it was not serious. This went on for a few weeks and Ron, Bruce and I kept in touch with each other by phone. On December the 22nd I phoned the old people's home to enquire how Mother was and the reply I got was, "Mrs. Dunkley died this afternoon and who are you?" I replied that I was her youngest son and that was not the way to speak to me.

I could not contact Ron at home, he and Joyce had gone to

stay with Janet for Christmas, so I phoned him there. I then phoned Bruce, who had just got home from work, and it was he who would have to go to Laindon to arrange Mother's funeral. We had to wait until 28th December for that, which took place in Colchester.

On Christmas Eve Margaret and I went to the midnight service at the Cathedral, but I could not get into the festive spirit in spite of my favourite hymns that were being sung. A very sad time for us all.

Mother's remains were taken to Plympton where they were interred on Father's grave on 9th January 1978, one day before what would have been Mother's ninetieth birthday. At the internment were Ron, Joyce, Winnie Moreton and her husband, Joe, and daughter, Julie, and some of the parishioners who had known Mother. I for my part was still out of work and money was very short, so I did not go to Plympton for the internment.

With my redundancy money I had paid off the mortgage on the house so that eased the situation, not to have to worry about having a roof over our heads any more, which left the rates, gas, water and electricity, and phone bills to pay. We got around this by using the budget scheme for most of the bills which my Post Office pension paid for.

I had applied for National Assistance as it was then, but I was refused any help because, between Margaret and myself, we jointly had money above the minimum limit. So I said to the lady who had come to see us, "Had I bought a car with my redundancy money and parked it around the corner, and wasted more on TV sets etc., would I have been eligible for financial help?" The answer I got was, "Yes!" I told her that that kind of thing was not in my book, I look after what little I have got. Try as hard as I could, I was unable to get any kind of job, mainly for two reasons, one was my age and the other was my disability. I still held my registered disabled card which should have helped me in getting employment, but it was to no avail. Prospective employers still held negative attitudes towards me, just exactly as it was when I first left home in 1952.

I kept myself busy helping Margaret as and when I could, and worked the allotment until, after I had my fork and spade stolen from the shed, I decided to give it up. Before I did this, we prepared the garden at home to replant the raspberry canes in late summer. I dug the ground over and made a trench which was filled with kitchen refuse. Then we built the frame and stretched the wires between the posts.

Early in May, Olive came to see us and took Margaret back to Chippenham to stay for a few days. On the Wednesday morning, while taking Kenneth to school, I fell down heavily on my right side and fractured my femur. John and Andrew came to the hospital and took Kenneth home with them and phoned Margaret to tell her what had happened. She was at the hospital by 2.00 p.m., where she found me in great pain. It was not until the Friday that I had the fracture pinned and plated and again it was another ten days after that before I went home. Kenneth would not go back to school until he could see that I was very much better. In all, it took a year before I was fully recovered from this fall.

In September, we dug up the raspberry canes from the allotment and planted them the same day in the back garden. From then on we have had a good crop of raspberries each June, upwards of thirty pounds. We ate some, froze some, and Margaret made jam with some as well, which was very nice in the winter.

We did not go away this year and stayed at home, but Margaret did go to see her parents in the summer months, and I believe her mother paid her fare for her. She also saw Olive and Betty; they came to see us and we were taken out to lunch.

Betty had also taken her redundancy pay but as she was older than me, she did not need to seek other employment.

We began to save a little sum of money each week during the year so that we could afford to have the kind of food and presents that we would like at Christmas time. We have kept the system going over the years, so we always can afford to have a good Christmas.

Margaret and I between us made tomato chutney from the tomatoes that I had grown; then we pickled onions and eggs. In October, Margaret made the Christmas cake and puddings, which she did each autumn. We considered that it was cheaper in the long run than buying the shop ones. In any case, ours tasted much better. Also in October, John began a course at the Technical School, which included work experience.

We had a fairly good Christmas, but money was still very tight, so we lived in the hope of me getting a job in the New Year.

With no prospects of another job, 1979 began with heavy hearts. I was signing on each week and if it had not been for my G.P.O. pension, we would not have been able to pay our way. The unemployment money just about covered our food and we walked everywhere as much as possible. Even Andrew's bus fare was getting to be a burden on our resources and I had not felt so depressed in my life, worrying how we were going to manage.

Margaret had not been too well and having been referred to a gynaecological specialist, she went to see him in April. It was decided that she needed to have a hysterectomy operation very soon. Margaret went into hospital early in May and had the operation. The day of the operation I was very worried about her and we could not see her until the evening, by which time she had been back from the theatre for about six hours. After spending ten days in hospital she came home for one night and the next day, she went to Clevedon to convalesce for three weeks. She was still not fully recovered when she came home and we had to keep the house going and look after her for at least another month. I am glad to say that she made a complete recovery.

John was still at the Technical College and Andrew was, by now, in his last year at school. Because Andrew's birthday was in December, he had to wait until the end of the summer term before he was able to leave school. This was not a very good time for any of us. John had completed his time at the Tech. in April, so now two of us were signing on at the Labour Exchange.

Andrew left school in June and joined John and me on the dole. There is nothing more depressing than to have three men from the same family all on the dole at the same time. However, this was not going to last for too long. Andrew got himself a job in the restaurant at Strensham Services, on the M5 motorway, but the wages were very low. Then two weeks later, I managed to get the clerical storekeeper's vacancy at Ronkswood Hospital. This work was very similar to managing a shop except that there was no money involved. I was responsible for keeping the stock of various equipment and toiletries etc. for the wards and all the other departments within the hospital.

Shortly after I began there, John got a permanent job with the city council, so at last, within less than two months, we had all managed to cease being unemployed. This was a great relief to all of us and we were now able to become more solvent than we had been for nearly two years. Andrew stayed working at the M5 service station until September, when he left to work as a porter at the Giffard Hotel, opposite the Cathedral. The pay there was very poor for the work that he was expected to carry out and sometimes he worked very late in the evenings. Eventually, he decided that he wanted to do better things with his working life so he was on the lookout to better himself. From now on, we hoped that we would never ever find ourselves in such a situation again.

Andrew began to think of taking a holiday on his own next year, but I was more concerned with getting the interior decorating done. Margaret and I began to plan what rooms would be done during the next year.

In the meantime, we also began to plan for Christmas by pickling eggs and onions, making chutney and cooking the Christmas cake and puddings.

Early in December, Olive and Betty arrived with their Christmas presents and we gave them ours. We were treated to lunch and, because of bad weather setting in, Olive decided to return home before it got too dark.

Christmas was a much happier time this year, in spite of Andrew being told he would have to work all day on Christmas Day from 6.30 a.m. until 9.00 p.m.. From his point of view, this was not being fair to him, so he told the head porter that he would only do it if he was paid triple-time plus three days off. This was refused, so he gave his notice in from that point and left the Hotel two weeks before Christmas.

On the first Thursday in January 1980, Andrew began working for an insurance broker in the city centre, and we began to look forward to better weather so that we could redecorate two bedrooms and the sitting room. Buying and storing the materials kept us very busy as well as the usual run-of-the-mill chores that needed to be done.

Towards the end of April I had a letter from Aunt Hilda telling me that she was staying in Aunt Anne's house in Southend-on-Sea because Aunt Anne was not very well and that she had been admitted to hospital. Aunt Anne became much worse as time went on and early in June, she died. The funeral was held a week later. I did not attend, but unknown to me I was expected to go. Ron, Joyce, Bruce and Celia went along with Aunt Hilda, and afterwards, Aunt Anne's will was read out. She had left me her house and some money as being the main beneficiary. My two brothers and three sons as well as neice Janet were included, but Bruce's two sons were omitted.

The first I knew about this was a phone call from Ron, telling me of my good fortune. He upset Aunt Hilda by his action because she wanted to be the one to tell me first.

For a time, feelings in the family were a little strained, to say the least. Both Ron and Bruce were left much smaller amounts of money and, because of it, Bruce especially felt very hurt about the will. Whereas Janet, John, Andrew and Kenneth were left some money, neither Alan nor Stephen were mentioned in the will. It was Bruce who had become the nephew to visit Aunt Anne, because he worked in Southend-on-Sea, he was expected to call and see her very often. This at times was impossible to do, with the volume of work which Bruce had to complete each day, which Aunt Anne would not or could not understand. She thought Bruce was at times making excuses not to visit her. So it was very hard for him to be left only a small amount of money, and nothing for his two sons. I felt very sorry for him at the time, and in later years, I did help him out when he needed it. After all, I had asked him for help in years gone by with the conservatory, which he would have given had he had the means at that time. So, in my own way, I tried to make up for what he should have had.

We had decided to decorate the sitting room after the dining room. Andrew helped in taking off the old wallpaper and then he went on his holiday. He had decided to travel to Europe on a camping holiday. He met up with a group of other people of his own age in London and he went from there to France. Their next stop was Belgium, then on into Germany. From there, he went to Austria and on into Italy. From there, they went to Monaco and the South of France. Their last place to visit was Paris, then back home to England.

On his return, we had just about finished putting the front room straight after the decorating. Wally Curnock from next-door had helped us with doing some plaster work on the chimney breast after renewing the damp course.

I had begun to write to Aunt Hilda more often since Aunt Anne's death, hoping to heal any bad feelings there might have been. Of all the nephews, Ron was the one who knew her best of all, whereas I hardly knew her. She was Father's youngest sister and they hardly kept in touch when Father was alive. However, I was invited to visit her for a few days in Broadstairs in Kent. I went to see her in October and as I now had sold Aunt Anne's house and I was much more financially solvent, I decided to travel first-class by rail to London, then on to Broadstairs from Waterloo Station. Her upper flat was quite near to the railway and each time a train went by, the building shook from the vibration.

The weather was not too good at that time of the year so we did not venture far during my stay. Aunt Hilda had a grandmother clock that was in the contents of Aunt Anne's house, which had been left to her. I took a fancy to it and offered Aunt Hilda twice what it was worth. She had had it repaired and it was valued up to £500, but she declined my offer.

On my return to Worcester, I told Margaret about the clock and her reaction was to say, "And where would you have put it had you bought it?" I could not answer that question.

The next journey we had to take was to celebrate the Golden Wedding anniversary of Margaret's parents. I had an order from Olive for six stools, so we took them on the train with us to Chippenham. There were upwards of fifty people there, some of whom had known them before they got married. The weather was much better now, being a brighter day. We stayed until late afternoon and Olive drove us to the station to catch our train.

With our new-found wealth, we began to look once more at larger houses because we felt that we had been at this house long enough and that we deserved a better one. We had seen a house in Athelstone Road, not far from here, which was a semi-detached, three bedroom with a separate lock-up garage. We had a discussion about the house and decided that we could make improvements to it and put in an offer, which was accepted. However, we had it surveyed and on the result of this, we decided to withdraw from the negotiations because, structurally, it was not a viable proposition.

We looked at further properties, but we thought it would cost too much, so we looked at and considered enlarging our own house. John, Andrew and Kenneth were now growing up fast and would soon be needing more space in their bedrooms. I had been aware of what I considered to be a reputable local builder and I had seen the quality of their recent work on properties nearby. They had been established for over one hundred years and the Lloyds Bank building on The Cross in the city centre was built by them in Victorian times. It was this firm that I had engaged to carry out the work. We had the house surveyed and we drew up plans of what we would require for everyone's benefit.

We now concentrated on getting organised for the coming festive season, and for Olive and Betty's annual visit with the exchange of presents, which was becoming a kind of ritual.

Christmas was celebrated in the usual way and both John and I had a week off from work.

Chapter Nineteen

CAUSE FOR CELEBRATION

Now that Christmas and the New Year celebrations were over, we concentrated on plans for a new extension. Before the work could begin, the plans had to be passed and it was early in the year that I was told that the house was in a conservation area. Therefore, the Council Planning Committee came to view the property. As the roof was to be renewed as well, I asked for it to be tiled and not slated. This was turned down by the Council, except that the extension could be tiled. I realised that it would give the roof an odd appearance, so it was decided on slating the whole roof. This added an extra £500 to the overall costs.

Work was to begin in early February and I was assured that the work would be completed by the end of May at the latest. This then would give us time to clean the house, re-arrange the bedrooms, decorate the enlarged one and repaint the kitchen before going on holiday. The plans were passed with the slight alterations to comply with the conservation area and work did start in February.

Each time I came home from work I inspected what progress had been made and if I was not satisfied, I drew the attention of the foreman to what I had noticed. Several times Margaret told me that the apprentice boys working on the alterations were not doing enough work, which was dragging the time out on the extension. I began to have shorter lunch breaks and arrived home earlier than expected. I heard a lot of laughing and joking one day and I asked Margaret what was going on upstairs. She said that they had been like that all day. I went to see what work had been done and realised very little had been done since the day before. I told the workers that I was not satisfied with the amount of work done in recent days, and as I was indirectly paying their wages, they had better get on with the work.

I phoned the builders' office and asked the foreman and director to come and see me that evening. When they came, I pointed out that we were not happy with the slow rate of progress and reminded them of the promise of the completion date, and that I wanted the foreman here more often to keep any eye on the men working. Things improved for a while but not as fast as we would have liked, and it was becoming a burden to us with the upheaval and inconvenience of the work. It was also realised that the conservatory foundations were inadequate, so it had to be pulled down and rebuilt, that was another unexpected expense of £500.

May came and went, followed by June and still there was no end in sight of the work being completed. By this time I was really getting frustrated as it was causing unnecessary bad feelings in the family. We were due to leave for our holiday on 18th July, to the Isle of Wight, for two weeks, and I wanted the work finished before then. I badgered the office as much as I could, but it seemed that they were unperturbed about the work. They were very quick in having me pay them a certain amount every month, but when I suggested that I would withhold the next payment, things began to happen.

When I left work on the Friday on the eve of our holiday, the painters were finishing off painting the front of the house and by the time that they cleared up, they did not leave until nearly 6.00 p.m., the work was over eight weeks beyond the completion date. This meant that we now had to face decorating the new extensions in the bedroom and kitchen after our holiday instead of before.

We hired a private car to take us to Southsea to catch the hydrofoil ferry to Reigate. We left here at 5.00 a.m., I had Kenneth on my lap in the front seat while Margaret sat between John and Andrew in the back seat. To say that we were cramped in this car, would be putting it mildly. In any case, we got to Southsea in time for the 9.00 a.m. ferry. At Reigate we caught the train on the pier for Shanklin where we were going to stay. We were in a non-smoking carriage, but some ignorant people ignored the sign until I threatened to pull the communication cord if they did not put their cigarettes out; they then extinguished their cigarettes.

We managed to get a taxi fairly quickly from Shanklin station and we got to the guest house just before lunchtime. After we booked in, we went to the main bus station and bought run-about tickets for us all. With these tickets, we were able to travel all over the island, so we made full use of them. We travelled over the island visiting the many villages and resorts and hardly a day went by when we walked either to Sandown or walked back to Shanklin. There is a cliff path to walk as well as a path along the sea shore, so we walked in each direction on which way that took our fancy.

We booked to see Jimmy Tarbuck, supported by Kenny Lynch, on the pier in Sandown and after the show, we walked back to Shanklin along the sea shore.

There was an American restaurant in Shanklin, so after our main evening meal at the guest house, we then went to the American restaurant for another three course meal. The portions were very large, but we battled through it and had a great evening. On our way back to the guest house, someone jokingly suggested fish and chips before arriving at the guest house.

We watched sticks of rock being made in old Shanklin village and brought some home. We also went to Godsall village where we bought a flagon of locally-made cider to bring home. The other places that we went to see were Osborne House, which had belonged to Queen Victoria but is now held in trust so that the public can see parts of it; and the other was Carisbrook Castle near Newport, which had held King Charles as a prisoner.

We enjoyed our stay on the island so much that we booked the same guest house for the following year for the same two weeks.

When we began our trip home by the same hired car, the driver took a wrong exit at a roundabout and he got lost. We insisted that he make a stop not once but twice so that we could get a drink and visit the toilets. In consequence, he moaned that he did not want to make a comfort stop as he said he was losing business and the journey was taking too long. At last, we arrived home much later than we planned and we had fish and chips for our supper. We had to make do with what food was available in the freezer for lunch on Sunday, because the shops were not open.

After everything had been settled and I finished paying the builder, I think we all agreed that had we known how long the upheaval was going to be, it would have been much easier and less frustrating and expensive if we had persevered and bought another property and sold this one. Anyway, as far as I was concerned, the good reputation that the builder once had by now had completely disappeared. I would never recommend them to anyone. Within ten years the firm was bought by a larger consortium and no longer exists.

Eventually, we did redecorate the bedroom which John and Andrew made full use of with the extra space and Kenneth moved into their old room. After that, Margaret repainted the kitchen walls, so we were now all nice and clean and back to normal once again. I returned to work and so did John and Andrew, but Kenneth still had another month at home before returning to school for the autumn term. In September, I had to have another toe fused because of it being twisted. I was only in hospital for two days, then I came home. It was another six weeks before the pin was removed.

I had decided to invest what money I had left from Aunt Anne's estate and I saw a firm of financial advisers' advertisement in the local evening paper. I went to see them and I was advised to invest the money in a Scottish company which promised to give a good rate of interest. So I signed up and invested most of the money that I had left. I kept a certain amount in other investments that I could get out very quickly in case of an emergency.

We now began to think of what to do for Christmas and likewise, save up for the next year's holiday. The chutney and pickling were soon followed by the making of the Christmas cake and puddings; then there were the cards and presents to buy.

This year, it was our turn to visit Olive and her parents to exchange Christmas presents and be treated to lunch, Olive having booked a table in a hotel in the country near Calne. She and Betty, both having cars, did the ferrying of us to the venue. Margaret's younger brother Hugh came down from St. Albans with his son and daughter, so it was a very large gathering this time. Margaret noticed that Hugh expected Olive to pay for everything, which was also noticed by other persons present. John, Andrew and I tried to get him to buy a round of drinks, but his excuse was that he had no money on him.

We returned home later that day by train and once again, arranged the last minute things to celebrate the festive season. We had a quiet but a very good Christmas and we were now looking forward to 1982 fast approaching us.

We now began to plan for our second holiday on the Isle of Wight, but this time we were going to go by train to Portsmouth to catch the ferry.

The other plans we had were how John would like to celebrate his coming-of-age birthday. We suggested an evening meal and asked whom he would like to invite. We drew up a list of names and there would be fourteen people at the meal.

Now that we had no more maintenance to be done to the house, we were able to concentrate on our holiday arrangements and the birthday party.

The train journey to Portsmouth was long and boring, but we got to Shanklin in the early afternoon. The three young men shared a bedroom in the guest house whereas Margaret and I had been offered a bedroom at the rear, in a kind of chalet-type building with only a toilet across the path which we had to share with the owners. We realised our mistake because this room felt damp and the mattress that we used was on a bench not far off the ground. Undeterred, we stuck it out for a week, and asked for a room inside the guest house. The owner was very apologetic but there was not one available, so it was take it or leave it.

We planned the holiday much better this time, in that we did not always stay together. Andrew and Kenneth spent a day at a car museum and aquarium; John went to the beach at Ryde and dug up cockles; whereas Margaret and I went inland to visit a glass works and a nursery to see what plants and vegetables were being grown. That evening, the guest house owner put the cockles in a bucket of water where they cleaned all the sand out of themselves, and then she cooked them for us all to try. I was not tempted to try them because I am not a great lover of fish, but Margaret, John and Andrew did have some.

One evening, we decided to split up again and this time, John and Andrew went off for a Chinese meal and Margaret, Kenneth and I booked a meal at the White House Hotel, which many years ago until about 1946 belonged to Margaret's paternal grandfather. Each summer, Margaret and her sister and brother spent their school holidays there with their grandparents, mother, uncles and aunts. Margaret told the staff of her connection with the hotel so she was invited to look around while Kenneth and I stayed in the restaurant. John and Andrew met us there later, then we went for a walk before going back to the guest house for a night-cap.

In the two weeks that we were there we visited and did the things that we could not fit in on our visit the previous year. We had a much better trip home than when we went, but we decided not to use that guest house again next time, if we decided to visit the island in the future.

The next event was John's twenty-first birthday, which was to be at a pub in Upton Snodsbury. The mini coach arrived to take us there so that we did not have to worry about drink driving for anyone. We had booked Margaret's parents, Olive, Betty, Uncle Raymond and Bruce and Celia in a guest house in Bath Road, which was only a few minutes away by car. The meal went off very well and everyone had a good time. John gave a speech at the end of the meal in which he thanked everyone for coming and making it a happy day for him. We then returned here in the coach and more drinks were consumed before we went our separate ways.

After all the celebrating had been done, it was back to work on the Monday for those who had to, a good time being had by all.

Now it was time for jam and pickle-making again which would lead us to Margaret's birthday in November followed by the Christmas celebrations.

We took Margaret out for a meal to celebrate her birthday and then, in December, we took Andrew out to celebrate his birthday, at which Olive and Betty came from Calne armed with the presents for the birthday and Christmas.

1983 began and I for one was looking forward to the approach of spring time which, for me, is the best time of the year. Andrew would be twenty-one in December so we had plenty of time to think about how we could celebrate the event.

But first there was another operation for me to face. For over a year, the first two toes on my right foot had been giving me a lot of pain, because they were bending the wrong way. It was decided that I needed to have them fractured and the joints fused together, being held in place by long stainless steel pins. I was in hospital for a week in February with my leg in plaster once again, which I had to put up with for six weeks. Everything went off all right and after the plaster was removed, I was able to walk without pain once more.

Shortly after my recovery, Margaret and I became more involved with the Swan Theatre. Margaret, John and Andrew were already involved with the Children's Theatre, held on each first Saturday of the month from September through to May every year. I had made enquiries about being a front-of-house steward and I was advised that if I had an evening suit, I could be put on the list, but that there were no permanent evenings for me to do at present unless someone failed to turn up. Eventually, I was offered the third Saturday of the month on a permanent basis. I was to partner a Mrs. Griffiths, who sold the programmes and I took the tickets. I did this a few times, then one evening in the bar, Mrs. Griffiths mentioned something about her late husband. I then asked her if he had been a doctor and when she said, "Yes," I told her that I had been his patient.

Mrs. Griffiths also told me that she was the chairman of the local Ladies Guild of the R.N.L.I. and persuaded me to join. I then discovered that there was to be a concert later that year in the Festival Theatre in Malvern which she was organising and that Iris Williams was the top guest entertainer.

I offered to make a rug with the design of the R.N.L.I. flag for the raffle. The Redicut wool firm made the design on canvas and supplied all the materials free. I in turn gave my services

196

free and made the rug. It helped to raise £700 on the raffle alone. While we had been making all the arrangements to get the rug made, Margaret Griffiths and I had been observed having these discussions by the front of house manager.

On a future Saturday he remarked to me that my "girl friend" was late turning up for duty. I said, "What girl friend? I haven't got one." He then said to me, "Mrs. Griffiths, isn't she your girl friend?" I said, "Certainly not," and walked away from him. Later that evening, I asked Margaret to see me at the end of the show and I related to her what the Manager had said to me, referring to her as my girl friend. To nip this in the bud, she offered and I agreed that she gave up doing that Saturday and that I would ask my wife Margaret to take her place. I saw the person who was in charge of the rota and he agreed to let my wife Margaret take Margaret Griffiths' place. So my next Saturday for duty, we both turned up for duty. The front of house manager was very abrupt towards Margaret and I asked him to be more civil to her. He was very surprised that Margaret Griffiths had given up that particular Saturday. Much later that evening, I told him that his remarks about Mrs. Griffiths to me the previous month had upset her and both my wife and me and that was the reason why she gave up that particular Saturday. That is how Margaret became a steward with me which we continued to do for many years to come. He was also so rude to another couple on another Saturday that they turned around and walked out of the Theatre.

In the following year that particular manager gave up the position, much to the relief of everyone concerned.

It was time now that we gave more thought to Andrew's forthcoming twenty-first birthday. As things turned out, we did not celebrate it in the way that we wanted to; we just had a family get-together with Olive and Betty for a meal.

During the Christmas period, we helped out quite a lot at the matinees for the Christmas play at the Theatre. How we managed it as well as preparing for Christmas beats me, but somehow we did it.

Chapter Twenty

AN AUSTRIAN HOLIDAY AND
WE LOSE A GOOD NEIGHBOUR

We had decided that for 1984, I would pay for a family holiday for the last time. All the boys needed to do was to save up their own money to spend. We were going to fly to Munich from Birmingham and then go by coach to Kitzbuhel in Austria.

During the summer months at work I had begun to find it increasingly difficult to walk the corridor of the hospital several times a day, delivering the goods to the wards and other departments. The corridor is almost a mile long from end to end, so it was at least a mile and a half to walk from the stores to the maternity wards and back again. I applied, through the hospital management, for more assistance from the porters' lodge to help me, but there was always some excuse for the help not forthcoming. There were times when I was struggling to carry out the deliveries when there were at least four, if not more, porters sitting in the lodge on duty, one of whom could have helped me at the time.

The orthopaedic surgeon that I had been a patient of since 1961 had now retired and he was a patient on Ward 10. I went to see how he was and he then asked me how I was coping in the hospital. I related to him my problem about the pain in my ankle and how I was not getting any relief from it. I told him that I was prepared to see a consultant in Harley Street, London, if necessary and he advised me to see another consultant here in Worcester. With this advice, I went to see my G.P. and he arranged for me to see the other orthopaedic consultant, first as a private patient then as an N.H.S. one. He put me on the sick list for a month. After staying at home and getting quite a lot of rest, the pains in my foot and back began to subside and I returned to work for a week before going on holiday. I did this so that I would not lose my holiday for being on the sick list.

We had our flying departure altered to the East Midlands Airport instead of Birmingham. This meant that we had to leave here at 2.00 a.m. on Sunday morning to go to Birmingham and pick up a minibus to take us from there to the other airport.

John and Andrew went to the Theatre on that Saturday evening to help with some stage work and it was well past midnight before they came home. I was getting more and more stressed out because of this and nearly making myself ill wondering how much longer they were going to be.

The taxi arrived and we set off for Birmingham at 2.00 a.m. as arranged. On our arrival there we had to wait for the minibus to take us on to the East Midlands Airport. We arrived there about 5.30 a.m. and we took off at 7.00 a.m.. We got to Munich at 9.00 a.m. European time. Again, we had to wait until all the arrivals had been completed before setting off at noon for Kitzbuhel.

The weather was very warm and we were able to buy cool drinks on the coach from an ice box on board. After our arrival we unpacked and went for a walk in the town to get to know where the shops were. We would be buying our food for lunch each day. The next morning we took a much longer walk around the town and Andrew was delighted to discover that he could buy a beer in a beer cellar at 10.00 a.m. if he wanted to.

We had booked six one-day trips for the two weeks that we were there, to include Kremmel Falls and to visit Salzburg, where some of the "Sound of Music" was filmed. We also went to view Mozart's house in another part of the city which we all found very fascinating and interesting.

One evening each week we went to a hotel in a town called Going, where we had inter-hotel skittle evenings made up of teams of six. This was great fun and the leader of a winning team had to drink a tot of Schnapps, followed by a litre of ale, without stopping while standing on a chair. During the second visit, I crushed two fingers between two bowls and bruised them badly; I had them packed in ice to stop the swelling.

Another night we went to a Tyrolean evening where the locals put on a very good show for us of various dances, yodelling and sketches. They were all wearing the costumes of the country.

We split up one day so Margaret, Ken and I walked up the mountain, stopping for lunch halfway up at a restaurant. There were magnificent views everywhere we looked, and after reaching the top, we came down by cable car. John went on a horse riding lesson for the day, and Andrew joined a group who were going to walk twelve miles through the mountains. He was awarded a badge to say that he had completed the walk. On another day, John decided to visit a sauna and he was surprised to see a young couple there completely nude, which was the custom there.

In Kitzbuhel there were two kinds of cable cars which could be used to reach the mountain tops, where we had lunch some days, and we could see across the mountains and into the valley below. There was an indoor swimming pool which we made full use of on the days that we had rain.

We also had a day trip to Innsbruck and went on into Italy to visit Vipitaino where we bought our wines, spirits and cigarettes to bring home. We also had to travel along one of the highest roads in the world leading in and out of Italy, called Europa Highway. It was so high that it was fitted with highwire fencing to stop anyone from committing suicide. That motorway was an experience in itself.

On another coach trip, we went up into the mountains to see the Gloss-Glockner Glacier, where only small coaches could be used. This was because the road had very sharp bends every few hundred yards or less, so it zigzagged across the mountain getting higher and higher. For me, this was very frightening and I could not bear to look where we were going; I was shaking like a leaf when we got to the top. Then we had to come down the same way, so it was necessary for the coach to have very good brakes. I was glad when we got back into the valley and I do not wish to have that experience again. There was a young baby in our coach who kept on being very tetchy and I suspect that it was feeling scared like me, because it was much better when we had come off the mountain. For the two weeks that we were there, we thoroughly enjoyed it except for me and that mountain trip.

We flew back to England getting home late on the Sunday afternoon. After unpacking, we went next door to see how Wally was and Lil, for whom we had brought presents. They had looked after our house while we were away. Wally was not very well and he was in a great deal of pain.

I returned to work the next day, as did everyone else, and Ken had the rest of the month at home on holiday.

At work there was quite a lot of paperwork to sort out and bring up-to-date in between delivering any goods to the wards and departments. I worked through my lunch break and at 4.00 p.m., I packed up and left at 4.15 p.m. and went home. The next morning I was summoned to the assistant adminstrator's office who wanted to know where I was after 4.00 p.m. the previous day, because the porter could not get into the stores to get an item. I explained that I had worked through my lunch break and had brought two weeks' paperwork up-to-date, and all I got was, "The next time you decide to leave early, get my permission first." I was also asked had I thought of retiring on health grounds, so I pointed out that I was registered disabled which meant that they should offer me alternative employment, more office work and less of the delivery side. The answer I got was that was not strictly true. So I replied,, "In other words, you have had your orders from higher up the chain to get rid of me." The answer I was given was, "Yes, in a roundabout way, that is the position."

This to me was all the thanks I got for working so hard on my first day back, and before I took my holiday, by coming off the sick list. I went to see my doctor the next day and he put me back on the sick list and asked me why had I gone back to work. It was only then that I found out that I could have my holiday while still being off sick, it would have been termed convalescence. I did not return to work after that. After having gone through yet another medical by the staff doctor, I was released from my employment on health grounds. In their eyes, being unable to carry out my work due to the polio in my leg and other side effects of hip and back pain from it.

During that week while all this was going on, Wally next door had been readmitted to hospital on the Tuesday and he died the following Saturday morning. This was a great blow to Lil and she was in a daze for several weeks after. We were quite affected by it, too, not knowing how Lil would now manage on her own.

I was now on sick leave with full pay for six months and on half pay for a further six months. So from that point of view, we had no financial problems.

I felt that I needed to do something which did not mean me being on my feet too much, so I began making more rugs and covering stool frames, mainly in the winter to keep myself occupied.

We had the usual autumn preparations towards Christmas and I was pleased that I did not have to get up early and travel in all weathers to work. On the other hand, I was concerned about the rest of the family having to do so.

Now that I was home all the time I went shopping with Margaret most days of the week, helping to decide what food we would require. I also began to take more interest in the kitchen by preparing the vegetables each Sunday morning for the lunch-time roast. (Little did I know, then, how this was to help me in later years to come.)

Socially, we began to get more involved with Children's Theatre at the Swan Theatre and eventually, we both joined the Swan Theatre amateur company. By this time, both John and Andrew had been members for several years. We began to help in the workshop, building and painting the sets for our plays, which were performed on the main stage four times a year. We would then help out at the weekend prior to the opening night. This work could take all day and most of the evening to make sure that everything was done to perfection so that the cast could have their final rehearsals. During the run of the plays, we would help out as stage crew backstage.

We nearly always went out for supper after the show was over, either to a Chinese or Indian restaurant during the run of the play. Then, on the last night, we had to strike the stage after the final curtain and leave it clear for the next professional production.

As you can see, this kept me very busy at times in the evenings and Margaret joined us to help towards the two weeks prior to the play opening night.

Margaret went to see her parents several times during the year. Her mother suffered very badly from arthritis and could not get about very well. Mr. Sharp took advantage of these visits and went away travelling by train to various parts of the country. He was very interested in trains all through his lifetime.

Chapter Twenty-One

FURTHER AFIELD

In 1986 Margaret and I were making plans to have a holiday on our own and we chose Ilfracombe to visit. We booked early in the new year so that we could get the hotel that we wanted. We had booked to go in August. Ken was now fifteen and with John and Andrew that much older, we felt it was about time that we left them on their own. However, I had other future plans of a different holiday in my mind at that time for the following year.

I had met several people when I had been out shopping with whom I had worked at the Hospital and who, like me, were now retired and they had joined the Retirement Fellowship of the N.H.S. and they asked me to join. After giving it some thought, I decided to join, so once every two weeks, we met in the social club at the Hospital.

We held a Christmas dinner each year at different venues, and in the summer, we would have coach trips to all sorts of places. Margaret would come with me on these trips which were either half or all day trips. One year we went as far as Windsor Castle and as near as Prinknash Abbey, in Gloucestershire. I was pleased that Margaret went on these trips, because it meant that she would have other ladies to talk to and it gave her a break from the housework.

In August, we went by train to Exeter where we changed and went on the single rail track to Ilfracombe. We booked into the hotel, but the room was very small for two people with just about enough room for both of us. We decided that we would take a walk and get our bearings so that we could get around fairly quickly.

However, the next morning I was ill with a very bad tummy upset which was gastro-enteritis. It would not abate at all, no matter what I took to remedy it, it soon came back again. The only soothing thing I could keep down was brandy. In the end, I decided not to eat the evening meal or breakfast the next day hoping, by starving myself, it might clear up. Talking to the hotel owner, I found out that fluoride was in the water and that many people staying there during the summer from the Midlands had the same problem.

We stuck it out for the week and on one day, I was well enough for us to take a trip on a boat around Lundy Island. Margaret enjoyed it so much that I said to her, "That does it; we are going on a cruise next year to celebrate your fiftieth birthday later in November and my sixtieth the following March." She was not too keen at first, so I said, "We will talk more about it when we get home."

We also managed trips to Westward Ho!, Barnstaple and Clovelly during our brief stay.

When we got as far as Exeter on our way home, it was only then that I began to feel much better and within a few days at home, my gastro-enteritis had cleared up; so I put it down to the fluoride causing it.

In the B.T. magazine I had seen an advert about a cruise for two weeks, starting on March 6th next year. I gave it to Margaret to read and asked her would she be interested. At first, she said that it would cost too much, but after some more discussions and a little persuasion, I sent away for the brochure and I suggested we look at it first before making a final decision. She agreed to this idea and, of course, John, Andrew and Kenneth all agreed that we should go, remarking that they would cope for two weeks on their own.

After reading the brochure and noting the cost involved, I thought that it was quite reasonable, but that I would cash some shares because I thought that this could be a one-off holiday.

Margaret still showed some doubts about it, but with a little coaxing from all of us, I sent off the deposit and booked the cruise.

It was now getting towards November and we were determined to give Margaret a birthday to remember. We booked a table at a restaurant, but I don't think the meal was all that good. It lacked quite a lot for what we paid for it.

Christmas was fast approaching and also the New Year which I for one was looking forward to with the cruise next spring.

After the Christmas and New Year celebrations, excitement began to grow with the forthcoming cruise in a little over two months' time. In the meantime, we had the winter weather to contend with, with very frosty mornings and being very cold. On the 6th March there was a ferry disaster in Zeebrugge, when the ferry turned on its side and there were many dead, injured and missing passengers.

The next morning, 7th March, Margaret and I left for Cheltenham by train to catch the coach which would take us eventually to Plymouth where the cruise ship would leave on the evening tide. It was very cold and after we got on the coach, we learnt from the lady coach driver that we were going to Cardiff first to pick up about twenty passengers, then cross the River Severn and join the M5 for Plymouth.

As we set off for Cardiff, it began to snow and gradually this turned into a blizzard on the M50 motorway, and we were reduced to travelling at 20 m.p.h.. When we got into Cardiff we were about ninety minutes late. The driver also had to contend with the vast crowds which had come for the England v. Wales rugby match. Several of the passengers moaned at being kept waiting for so long for the coach and they did not accept the reasons given by the driver until she asked those who had been on the coach from Cheltenham why we were late.

We set off for the M5 but first, we had to get through the crowds of rugby fans so it took at least an extra half-an-hour to get out of Cardiff. On reaching the M5 service station, we stopped for a break and the driver phoned the docks in Plymouth to inform them that our estimated time of arrival would be much later than planned. If we were too late to reach the ship, it would be delayed, which meant setting sail on the Sunday morning tide.

The weather changed from snow to rain when we joined the M5 westward towards Plymouth, so it was much quicker and the driver had a chance to catch up on lost time. We made a quick comfort stop at Exeter, by which time it was getting on for late afternoon and now the sun was shining. So from Cheltenham to Exeter we had travelled through a blizzard, rain, sleet, fog and sunshine, quite a mixture of weather to start a holiday cruise with.

We were only an hour late in reaching Plymouth and we were soon all aboard and finding our cabins. We left the harbour on time and by 7.00 p.m., we were sitting down to our first four-course meal of the cruise. At our table we had eight persons and only two of us were men. The other man was a retired policeman accompanied by his wife, and four ladies, two who had been on a quite a few cruises together, and the other two were friends; one was single and worked at Marks & Spencers in Cheltenham, and the other was married. Except for Margaret and me, they all lived in and around Cheltenham.

The Channel was calm as we sailed towards the Bay of Biscay and Cape Finisterre.

The meal was excellent and it made up for the bad coach trip to Plymouth. After the meal, we went to one of the lounges where we were entertained by a singer and a pianist for an hour. We then toured the ship, getting our bearings and sea legs, and found the lounge where the stage was and the main entertaining area. We could have another meal at midnight, if we wanted it, which was available throughout the cruise. On a lower deck there was a disco for the younger generation, but we decided not to avail ourselves of that.

The next day, Sunday, we had posted in our cabin door the events of the day, ending with the Captain's cocktail party. Evening dress was to be worn for that event to meet the Captain and the senior officers, which was followed by the evening meal. After that we had a cabaret where the stewards waited at the tables and served the drinks that we had ordered.

Crossing the Bay of Biscay was rough as a ridge of low

pressure advanced towards us. The next morning it was still stormy so the Captain ordered full-steam-ahead at 18 knots. Forty passengers had been injured but we made good time and we sailed into Lisbon at 1800 hours, twelve hours ahead of our estimated time.

At breakfast that morning we got talking to a couple who remarked about the passengers' trip from Cheltenham and we told them that we were on that coach. When I enquired how far they had come from, the lady replied, "Crownhill," and I said, "I know where that is; it is part of Plymouth on the road leading to the moors and Tavistock." When she said, "How do you know that?" Margaret replied, "Norman was born in Plympton." The lady then said, "Did you know anyone called Bill Stanmore?" and I said, "Of course I do, I grew up with him and he was one of my school friends." Then she said, "He is my Uncle." I then replied, "Wait a minute. What was your maiden name?" and when she said, "Whyat," I told her that the last time I had seen her was when she was a little girl when I had called at Bill's house because we were going out that evening and she wanted to come. What a small world this was turning out to be!

Bill, being the youngest of the family of six and one of his sisters was the mother of this lady. She was celebrating her twenty-fifth wedding anniversary. We knew there was a photographer on the ship and each evening, we could buy any photos that he had taken which were on display in a small shop. At £1 each, we began to collect quite a few photos and this was besides the ones we would be taking ourselves.

Each morning a list of the day's events, such as keep fit classes, dancing lessons, bingo and clay-pigeon shooting, were posted through the cabin door, so it was up to the individual whether or not to take part.

When at sea we nearly always played bingo in the afternoons when tea was served at 3.00 p.m.. Food, there was plenty of variety and plenty of it and the displays that we saw we had never seen before. They were quite an art in itself.

The weather was warm enough to sunbathe on deck as we sailed towards Lisbon, but we kept to small doses of that. In the evening after dinner, we went for a stroll on deck before we went to another cabaret at 10.30 p.m., which went on past midnight. We got quite a serene and tranquil feeling in the evening air strolling on the deck in evening dress, so we did it most evenings.

On Tuesday after breakfast, we went on a coach tour of old and new Lisbon and we walked through some very narrow streets where small shops were open, but to us it seemed another world away. From there, we went to the seafront and were taken to see horsedrawn coaches of a bygone era of the last century which the Portuguese Royal Family used along with heads of state. We finished up in a wine lodge to taste a glass of local wine. We were able to buy a bottle as well.

After lunch on the ship, we went to Sintra by coach, passing through the orange and lemon groves to visit the well-known castle there, where Prince Charles and Princess Diana had stayed. The pungent aroma from the groves was very strong, but pleasant. From there, we went on to Estoril before returning to the ship. Estoril had some magnificent gardens surrounding the casino, where we were able to walk while eating icecreams.

We left Lisbon behind on the evening tide and set sail for Madeira. We were at sea all day Wednesday, when everyone took advantage of the warm sunny weather and we all had a relaxing day. The food was absolutely wonderful and there was so much that we could keep going back for more if we wanted to. After another four-course dinner in the evening, we relaxed in the lounge to await the cabaret, which was followed by dancing.

Early next morning we arrived in Funchal, the main port on Madeira, and watched the ship being taken into the harbour and tying up. Here, we could make phone calls home after 6.00 p.m., which had to be booked in the morning.

We booked two half day coach trips. The first was to visit the botanical gardens and to get there, we had to go through winding roads up into the mountains. The coach was a very old one, and after we had gone on the basket run, the coach broke down and we had to wait for another one to take us back to Funchal, to a wine lodge before going back to lunch on the ship. The wine lodge walls were covered in blue and white tiles, depicting the wine-growing areas of the island.

After lunch, we went to Camancha to see the basket factory. What a sight this was to behold, from very minute miniature items upwards to very large furniture, all made from canes grown on the island. When we left there, we went to visit a shop in Funchal full of lace made locally, and after that, we had another visit to the same wine lodge, where we bought a bottle of Madeira wine.

When we got back to the ship, Margaret went on board while I made a phone call home. In Worcester, the weather was still cold and the snow was still lying in parts, but other than that, they were all coping all right while we were away.

We left Madeira on the evening tide and set sail for Tenerife, arriving early the next morning at the port of Santa Cruz. On the dockside there were tons of boxes of tomatoes waiting to be loaded for export.

After breakfast, we went on a coach trip to Puerto de la Cruz, passing through banana plantations. There were many night clubs and casinos there, which did not interest us. We left again in the evening to sail to Las Palmas. Here, we had a day trip around the island and at lunchtime, there were twelve different starters to choose from. This was followed by a veal or fish course and we could drink as much wine as we could manage.

When we sat down for lunch, a lady on her own was already sitting at the table. After introductions, we learnt that her name was Ivy and she was convalescing from shingles. When she got back to England, she was moving from the Home Counties to live in Worcester. We had more conversations with her on the coach for the rest of the tour of the island.

During the rest of the trip we paid a visit to a Catholic church which was richly decorated in gold. We had travelled up into the mountains and we had a panoramic view of the port as we got nearer to Las Palmas. That night at sea we had a barbecue and sangria party on deck at midnight, but the rain curtailed some of the programme so it ended earlier than arranged.

We were now on our way to Casablanca in Algeria and at 3.00 p.m., we were one hundred miles west of Agidare. We knew this because we managed to be picked for a visit onto the bridge of the ship. The ship had three radars on the bridge and we were fascinated to see the view of the sea from this position and we could make out the curve of the world on the horizon.

It was too hot to sunbathe so for a while, we watched the turtles swimming in the direction of Algeria. More entertainment was given after dinner that evening, but it was still too hot. The next morning, we arrived in Casablanca. Here, we booked a coach trip to Rabat to see the King's Palace. Before leaving the ship we had to surrender our passports to the local police, which we were not pleased about; they looked a surly lot and I did not trust them. I left all my money on the ship and I kept my watch inside my shirt. The ladies hung their handbags around their necks and hid them inside their clothing. We had been warned about pickpockets.

On the quayside were six coaches waiting for us and as each one filled up, we left the docks. I was feeling very nervous about this day out, but at least we were going to see how another country lived. We noticed on the way that the people of Algeria used the side of the road as a toilet. We were guided to a toilet in the suburbs of Rabat which was a dark room with no lighting with just a hole in the centre of the room. The ladies toilet wasn't any better; Margaret's description was more or less like the one we men used.

After seeing the King's Palace from the outside, we were taken to a restaurant for lunch. This was clean and airy and our plates were loaded with salad but very little meat. Wine was bought by the bottle for the meal or there was bottled water. After lunch, we arrived outside the casbah and as we left the coach to wait for the guide, we noticed this group of children, aged no more than three to ten. After we came out from the casbah, they were still there. We then had to walk up a hill and get back on the coach. It was here that we saw a very tall Arab in a very colourful costume, who turned out to be a water-carrier selling water. I managed to take a photo of him before we left. As we left, we looked out of the window and noticed the same group of children standing in a circle showing each other what they had picked from pockets that day.

When we got back to Casablanca, we were offered a visit to a large shop. I flatly refused to leave the coach along with two ladies. I had seen enough and I preferred to get aboard ship as soon as possible. However, the coach driver took us to a parking area in the middle of a very wide road for about an hour before going back to pick up the rest of our passengers to return us to the ship.

That evening, back on board ship, we had a full Greek menu for dinner and I did not eat very much. I was wary of what I saw on the menu. Unfortunately, some of the passengers were taken ill as a result of over-indulgence, but no one at our table was taken ill. Another concert followed after dinner and also in another bar there was an impromptu singalong with actions.

We were now on our way to Gibraltar, which most of the passengers were looking forward to and we were advised to put our watches forward by one hour that evening before going to bed. On Tuesday, we arrived very early in the morning and we toured the caves and went on to see the Barbary apes. This was done by taxi where most of the people spoke either Spanish or English. We were dropped off in the town at lunchtime which gave us about five hours for sightseeing and shopping. We mostly did sightseeing and a little shopping. We went to see a copy of the charter where it was mentioned how Britain obtained the Rock and that it was our property from that day forward for ever. It could not be taken from us. We also went to see the parish church which had mementoes of days gone by of previous battles, such as the Sir Francis Drake era. We were due to set sail for Plymouth at 6.00 p.m., so we got a taxi back to the ship. It was rather a long walk which passed beside the airport and border into Spain.

At sea on Wednesday there were various activities to do or just laze about. There was to be a fancy-dress dance that evening and there were sixty-four entrants. Prizes were won for different types and age groups and we had yet another late night.

Thursday, we were caught in Force 8 winds with the sea very rough, passing Finisterre at 6.00 a.m.. The farewell cocktail party had to be cancelled because there were too many ill with sea sickness. The ship was rolling fore and aft and one lady was injured. Dinner tonight was par excellence in spite of the weather, but we retired early knowing that we would be entering the English Channel the next day. Because of the rough seas, lying in my bunk I kept sliding up and down, so sleep did not come easily to me.

We entered the Channel on Friday at 9.00 a.m., passing the Lizard and we got to the Eddystone Lighthouse about 2.00 p.m. and dropped anchor at 3.30 p.m. in Plymouth Sound. Dinner was again a four course meal and we had a farewell party that night, which did not finish until well after 2.00 a.m..

We awoke to find that we were already tied up in Millbay Docks and we left the ship at 10.30 a.m.. We left the Dock about 11.00 a.m. and stopped for lunch on the M5 at 1.00 p.m. near Taunton. After an hour, we went on to Cardiff and it was much quieter this time than when we were there two weeks beforehand. We arrived back in Cheltenham at 4.30 p.m.. The retired policeman had arranged for his daughter to drive us home from there and we arrived home by teatime.

This was a holiday that would remain one of the happiest that Margaret and I had ever had. It was worth all the extra expense and as I said to Margaret, it was possible that it was a one-off, but if we could, it would be nice to do it again. I was certainly going to do so. We then had to get our films developed to see if they did the holiday justice, and they certainly did. We had many a laugh about some of the results. Now it was down to earth and getting back into the old routine once more.

John and Andrew were planning to visit Guernsey the following spring, but as for us, we decided that we would stay at home. We continued keeping the garden tidy and doing what we could at the Theatre a few evenings a week.

We had a day coach trip to Powys Castle which was very interesting and enjoyable, with a coffee stop on the way there and a tea break on the way back.

We paid a visit to Chippenham to tell Margaret's parents of our cruise and show them the photos which we had taken. Then it was back home again to get ready for the autumn and winter season at the Theatre.

I gave a talk to the Retirement Fellowship about the cruise

one week after I had got all the relevant photos and brochures and any menus that I had managed to obtain from the stewards.

Ken finished school in July and from September, he was going on to the Technical School for further education for a year. His ultimate goal was to join the ambulance service. He was given day release once a week, when he helped out on an ambulance on emergency calls. This made him all the more keen to join and he would not be happy until the Technical year was over.

We were now looking forward to Christmas and the New Year, and John and Andrew had booked a holiday for a week in Guernsey the following spring.

Olive came on her own this time just before Christmas, Betty was not very well and she only stayed a few hours before returning to Calne.

John had a week off from work, but Andrew was expected to only get the two days off, and they both finished early on Christmas Eve. Christmas was a quiet affair and Margaret and I were stewards on Boxing Day afternoon at the Theatre. I told Margaret that I would not be keen to do that again the following year.

* * * *

John and Andrew were looking forward to their holiday in Guernsey and left by air from Birmingham shortly after my birthday. At that time of year, there is very little public transport on the island, so it was either walk or book a taxi. They had a great time at the hotel where they were staying and when they got back, John said that because of the walking that they did, he was going to take up driving and buy a car. This was a great surprise to us because, up to then, we had never thought about having a car.

They had stayed at the Flying Dutchman Hotel and they were so well looked after that we booked a two weeks holiday for the following June. We had also booked a holiday to Oban that we saw advertised in the local press. It would not be until the end of October and we would arrive back on Margaret's birthday.

Kenneth's next day release was to Ronkswood Hospital and to my amazement, he had to deliver the goods from the store that I had been in charge of and he was not paid for it. Talk about cheap labour. There was I, less than a year before, asking for more help which was refused and that I was pensioned off; now my own son was doing my old job for nothing. I was livid when Ken told me what he was doing, but there was nothing that I could do about it now.

During the summer we had a good harvest of raspberries and tomatoes, which we made full use of. We made more chutney and jam and I was getting still more involved in the kitchen. I was beginning to prepare meals and cooking them. Margaret was there to advise me when it came to making pastry and cakes and some of my efforts turned out all right, but to start with I had many failures. I was not cooking the Sunday joint, which Margaret was still doing, but the rest of the preparations I could do.

We left here on a dull, wet October Saturday and we were driven to Kidderminster and Stourport to change coaches and driver. We seemed to be travelling for hours and not getting anywhere, making several comfort stops on the way. We eventually arrived in Gretna Green about teatime where we had a much longer break; so we visited the famous anvil and the souvenir shops close by. We set off again skirting around Loch Lomond on a very nasty narrow road with many bends in it. We then made another stop where "Take the High Road", the TV programme, was filmed. Margaret was pleased about this because she had followed the story on the TV.

We arrived in Oban well after dark and the driver did not know where the hotel was situated, so that was another delay. We eventually found it at about 7.00 p.m. after having left Worcester at 8.30 a.m., a very long day's travel and we were all tired.

The next day was a free day so we went sightseeing around the harbour and the hills behind Oban, where there was a folly to see. On Monday, we did a day tour to Fort William and back, travelling through the valleys and seeing the salmon fish farms and wild salmon in the rivers. The weather was atrocious, nothing but rain most of the time, so we could not see very far into the mountains and valleys. It was so bad that it blotted out the top of Ben Nevis. The next day we had a morning trip to the small coastal village of Inveraray where we had coffee before returning to Oban for lunch at another café. There is a whisky distillery in Oban so, to get away from the rain, we went on a tour to see that and we finished up having a wee dram of single malt whisky. Then we went into the shop where the product was sold. We bought a bottle to bring home with us.

The next morning, we were taken by coach to catch the ferry to the Isle of Mull; the weather was still not very good with still squally showers. On arrival at the island, we went by coach to the other end of the island, where we caught a very small ferry to the island of Iona. Here, we were able to walk to the Cathedral and then walk around part of the island, and we had lunch in a small café there. Opposite were a few shops selling groceries, fruit and vegetables. One was a souvenir shop with all manner of things relating to Scotland as a whole.

One of the coach drivers with us was there from Plymouth with a coach load from Devon, and he was introduced to me. We had a conversation about Devon and Plymouth in particular while we waited for the ferry to come and pick us up.

We returned to Oban, via the ferry again, and we arrived back in time before the shops closed.

Each evening the locals would come into the bar of the hotel and we were entertained by them. On one such evening we had a local organ player and an accordion player to entertain us along with a comedian. Then about 10.00 p.m., six ladies came in and ordered five double whiskeys and one soft drink. They sat quietly in the corner at first until someone asked them to give us a song. Well, to our amazement, these six ladies had wonderful voices and the party atmosphere was beginning to come alive. They then asked someone at the bar to sing a song and he sang us a song in a rich tenor voice. We found out later that they had been to choir practice being members of Oban Orpheus Choir. This went on until about midnight, but it did make up for the poor weather. Outside it was still raining.

The next day, we were off again on another coach trip, this time travelling across from west to east, then south again to a town on the banks of Loch Fyne. Here, we saw a real court of years gone by with dummies of the judge and jury and of the accused and plaintiff.

On our last night in Oban there was to be a ceilidh at the other end of the bay in a public building. The rain was being blown across the bay from the sea and we got very wet getting there. However, when we got inside the fun began at about 9.00 p.m. and everyone was letting their hair down. Various members from the audience were persuaded to get up on stage to entertain everyone with either stories, songs and playing the fiddle or accordion. Many had travelled as far away as Aberdeen and other towns in that area to be in Oban that night. Then, to my surprise, who should walk in and sit behind us were the six ladies who had entertained us at the hotel a few nights before. We got talking to them and that is when I found out that the one on soft drinks did the driving that night; so they took it in turns to drive, going out most nights visiting pubs and hotels, entertaining when asked to do so. There was a bar there and at 11.00 p.m., stovies, a well known Scottish dish, was served at £1 a plateful. This was very good and helped to keep out the cold. When I asked one of these ladies at what time the evening would finish, "Oh," she said, "any time between now and four o'clock next morning." I said, "What about going to work the next day?" and she replied, "They just get up and go, no problem." After this, we stayed on until midnight then we left to battle against the wind and rain across the bay back to our hotel.

The next morning we set off for Worcester at 8.30 a.m., stopping at Gretna Green for lunch. Here, the driver was able to get us tins of shortcake at a reduced price because of the amount that he ordered.

We travelled all day back to Stourport, a long tedious journey where, unknown to us, the driver was leaving. He just left the coach and he did not bid us goodnight. After waiting nearly half-an-hour we were all getting frustrated; then we found out that we were waiting for the other coach driver. We were very late getting back to Worcester, where we were met by John, Andrew and Kenneth. We came home by taxi, dumped everything indoors and went out to the restaurant for an evening meal to celebrate Margaret's birthday.

We were both very tired after such a long day and we were not sorry to be home and get a good night's rest.

Kenneth had been on a YTS scheme for over six months and now he had been accepted into the Ambulance Service, working at the control unit. This is what his aim had been since before leaving school.

Andrew's birthday was the next celebration, then it would be Christmas followed by the New Year.

John took his second driving test in November and he passed; he would start looking for a car in the New Year or spring time. He had begun karate lessons and he was getting along fine, but one evening he fell the wrong way and fractured his wrist. It was put in plaster for six weeks so he was unable to go to work for that time. This did delay him buying a car, but at least when he would get one, the weather should be a lot better.

Christmas and the New Year were celebrated in the usual manner and now we could look forward to a new beginning again.

Chapter Twenty-Two

A PLAY PREMIERE AND A CHANNEL ISLAND HOLIDAY

Having booked a holiday at the Flying Dutchman Hotel in Guernsey for the following June, I had now booked a flight with Midland Airways, so all we wanted now was to have good weather after the experience of the very wet week that we'd spent in Scotland.

There were more talks at the meetings each fortnight at the N.H.S. Retirement Fellowship and arrangements of more coach trips in the summer. Again, the weather seemed to be against us this year, being a very wet spring and not much drier as summer approached.

At the Theatre, Margaret, Andrew and I had been asked to be in the world premiere play of a book transcribed by David Goodland called "A Child in the Forest" by Winifred Foley. We began rehearsing in February nearly every night and at weekends, and we had three hymns to learn. It was first performed on Thursday March 9th and went on until March 25th. During the run, Winifred Foley came to see the matinee and all the cast met her for tea in the Theatre café afterwards. She gave us all signed copies of her book and she was delighted with our portrayal of her childhood.

David Goodland became a good friend to all of us and most of the professional cast were very good friends. We held a party after one of the performances and everyone had a good time; it was one of the best periods that we enjoyed at the Theatre. We were all sorry when it had to end. The play was such a great success that we had to do extra performances not to disappoint too many people. A sketch from it was recorded for a TV programme which was shown while the production was still on. Some of the cast came back to act in other plays later on. "Blithe Spirit" was one such play.

It was now nearing the time for Margaret and I to think about our holiday, but the weather was still not the good weather that everyone wanted. However, someone must have been smiling on us because the day of our departure in mid-June the sun came out and for the next two weeks that we spent in Guernsey, it was sunshine all the way.

We flew from Birmingham Airport and after one hour's flying, we arrived in Guernsey. We took a taxi to our hotel and then settled in to get to know the hotel area. We were made to feel very welcome and we met other guests from Devon, Holland and Germany. The restaurant was large and the food was good, and some of the staff were very helpful.

On the first Sunday we went into St. Peter Port and got ourselves a weekly ticket to use on the buses. While we were there we met a member of the staff from the Theatre here in Worcester. We went on a trip around the island to consider what places to visit for much longer and possible places for Margaret to have a swim. We were determined to visit all the other islands while we were there, so we had mapped out a busy time for ourselves.

We went to a tomato farm to see how they are grown on a commercial scale and while we were there, we bought a picture of partridge taking flight.

We saw the result of the German occupation during the War and saw the hospital, which had been built for the Germans by prisoners of war from Poland, Russia and other eastern parts of Europe. Margaret was more astounded at what we saw than I was, because during the War, she was living with her parents in Shiraz in Persia from 1938 to 1945, so she did not know very much about what happened in Europe, only that there was a war on at that time.

The next day we went to Herm Island and I surprised Margaret by walking all around it with her. It was about three to four miles altogether, but at least we took our time stopping very often because the day was very hot and sunny. Getting off and on the boat at the jetty was a bit awkward, but somehow we managed it all right.

Each evening before going into dinner I made sure I had a drink of whisky and Margaret had a sherry. One evening, I had rather too much and I had to be assisted to the restaurant. However, I made sure I did not do that again. The hotel had an outdoor swimming pool and we spent a few afternoons there, as a way to relax, because it was real summer weather and very hot.

Our next outing was to visit a craft centre where all manner of things were being made, including a glass factory. There was plenty to choose from so we bought a few gifts to bring home.

Our next island that we visited was Sark and here, I had my first taste of riding in a horse-drawn cart. Although, when I was growing up in my formative years and being surrounded by farms, I had never ridden in such a vehicle. On this ride we were taken to the other end of the island where we walked on the causeway that was built by the German prisoners of war at the end of hostilities in 1945. We also went around the gardens of the largest house on the island where the Dame of Sark lived during her lifetime on the island.

Each evening after dinner there was entertainment in the bar, if you could call it that. We were not very impressed with what was on offer so we stayed in the lounge talking to the other guests.

Our next trip was to the island of Alderney on the Sunday, midway between our two weeks' stay. We travelled in a hydrofoil for this, which was quite a new experience for us. We went to see the parish church, mainly to get away from the heat of the day. After that we saw where a memorial near to the harbour had been erected by the islanders in memory of those prisoners who had died digging tunnels for the Germans.

While we were waiting for the ferry to take us back to Guernsey, we saw two or three personalities who were now living on the island. One of them was John Arlott, the cricket commentator for the B.B.C. radio, who also wrote for one of the leading national newspapers.

The next day we took it easy and just went around the island by bus, only getting off to sit in the sun and eat our sandwiches that we had with us. I remarked to Margaret that I was thirsty and Margaret replied, "Look, there is a café and bar over there about five minutes walk away. Why don't we go there?" So we walked over and we went in and ordered our drinks and went and sat down by a table. A lady approached us with a menu card and I said that we had only come in for a drink. Whereupon we were given funny looks because she said, "You are sitting in the restaurant area." So I whispered to Margaret, "Drink up, we are not welcome here." As we were walking out a man sitting down with his elbows on his knees holding a newspaper in his hands looked up and stared at us. It was not until we were on the bus going back to St. Peter's that I realised it was Oliver Reed, the actor, who had stared at us. We found out at the hotel that he part-owned the café where we'd had the drink.

We had decided to leave going to Jersey as the last island to visit. We hoped that this was going to remind us of a lovely honeymoon which we spent there in 1960. However, times change and so did the island. There was very little that we could remember from twenty-nine years before. It was much more commercialised, aimed at the holiday trade which we were not pleased to see. We saw the Zoo which was now part of the attractions on the coach tour that was included and we finished in a souvenir shop which had all manner of gifts and there was a very large café there.

During our return by sea to Guernsey, the ferry fouled some fishing lines with its turbine twin screws, so we had to wait until it was freed. We were very late getting back to port and to the hotel, but we were able to get our evening dinner all right.

The beauty of Guernsey was that it was still unspoilt by the razzmatazz commerce of Jersey. There is a famous castle at St. Peter Port and it was open a few hours a day to visitors. So, on a not too bright a day, we toured this castle which was full of history, and how it was involved during the German occupation in the Second World War. Luckily, the Germans did not do too much damage to the islands, but what damage had been done most of it had been renovated.

We left the island and flew back to Birmingham Airport where we caught the train to New Street Station, where we caught the connecting train to Worcester.

The weather turned nasty after our return with more rain, so it meant that we might lose some of our raspberries. However, we picked them as and when we could and Andrew had picked quite a few while we had been away, so we did not lose too many.

For the rest of the summer, the weather was very unsettled so we had been lucky in our weather while in the Channel Islands. That had been the only two weeks of good weather this year, of being fine and dry with long sunny intervals.

We now saw an advert in the local press for a holiday in Austria by coach for 1990. I sent away for the brochure and we had several dates to choose from, the last one being in October. We booked to go in September the following year, but only Andrew was interested in going with us.

We had all the usual autumn work to do with preparing the cake and puddings, and pickling to do for Christmas, so Margaret and I were kept very busy. Margaret paid a visit to see her mother and stay with her while her father once again took a long train journey to Scotland and back in about seventy-two hours. Of course, this was no real rest for Margaret, she did quite a lot of cleaning in the house and tidied up the garden while she was there. She would only phone me from a local phone box rather than use her mother's phone; this was to keep the calls private, and her mother did not like me phoning Margaret; why this was I will never know.

On her return, we began to get ready to celebrate Andrew's birthday to be followed by Christmas and the New Year. We carried out our duties at the Theatre and we had the annual front-of-house staff party, which was the Theatre's way of thanking us for our work during the year.

We had also realised that 1990 was to be a special year for us because we would be celebrating our thirtieth wedding anniversary (our Pearl).

We began 1990 thinking of ideas of how we would like to celebrate our special day in August. Andrew, for the past year or so, had been working in a café at Callow End on Sundays where they served the traditional three-course English roast beef at lunchtimes. The owners were friends of the family and it was suggested that we have a buffet meal there on the Saturday, the 4th August, two days before the actual anniversary date. We would arrange at a later date what to put on the menu. So the café was booked and we began to look forward to the celebration by working out a guest list.

I had been gaining quite a lot in my weight so the doctor arranged for me every six weeks or so to have my weight and blood pressure checked at the surgery by the nurse. I had changed my eating and drinking to a certain degree and, over the months, my weight gradually went down and continued like that for several months.

There was a feeling of high activity during June and July as we approached our Pearl wedding anniversary. The invitations had been written and sent out and we made sure that those involved with our wedding in 1960 would not be missed out. However, Janet, my niece and bridesmaid, was unable to come so were Ron, Joyce, Bruce, Celia and Stephen. On Margaret's side, her parents came with Olive and Betty, so on the day of the party we had nine people sitting down to lunch. Andrew was busy with his and my cameras taking photos, mainly of Margaret and myself.

We all left in two cars early that evening because we had to greet all the guests who began to arrive by 7.30 p.m.. John, Andrew and Kenneth bought bottles of champagne and the café owners made the cake as a present. We had many gifts and everyone seemed to be enjoying themselves. Margaret's father wanted to leave at 10.00 p.m., but Margaret and Olive made him stay longer. They had to get back to Chippenham and Calne, so they left about 11.00 p.m. in the end. The day had been very warm and quite a few of us went outside in the late evening air where there were large candles lit to keep the moths and flies away. We eventually left for home about 1.00 a.m., having had a very long day.

On the Monday we had two requests played on the local B.B.C. radio by two of the presenters that we knew.

The next month, Margaret, Andrew and I left Worcester at 3.00 a.m. on a Saturday morning to start our coach holiday to Austria. Because we booked so early, we had the front seats in the coach, which we enjoyed immensely. We had to make pick-ups in Gloucester then Stroud and as we left Stroud, waiting at the traffic lights, we saw a fox just stroll across the road in front of us. We got to Ramsgate well in time for the ferry and after boarding it, we made for the restaurant for a meal.

After leaving the ferry at Calais, we made for northern France, where we would be stopping overnight at Nantes near the Franco/German border. The next morning, we left before 9.00 a.m. and travelled into Germany. We made a stop at a petrol station for more petrol and the coach had a wash, mainly to clean the windscreen. The views that we had from the front were at times breathtaking when going down into the valleys. Our final destination was St. Anton and the driver was not too sure how to get there. After crossing into Austria, he made a stop at a service station and made a phone call. I took this opportunity to make a comfort call.

When we got to within five miles of St. Anton, the driver was still uncertain as to which way to go. He had the choice of straight on or turn right and go through the mountain pass. He chose the latter and it was a very long tunnel that we went through. At the other end he had to pay a heavy toll for using that route. Entering St. Anton, he could not find the hotel at first until he made enquiries at a café. The hotel was up the top of a long hill on the outskirts of the town. On reaching it, he was asked why had he come the long way round. Had he kept straight on instead of turning right, he would have saved having to pay the toll using the tunnel.

The next day was a rest day so that we could explore the town. Being high up in the mountains made it awkward for me, but there was a taxi run by the hotel, so I used that very often.

The next day the coach took us to Liechtenstein and then on to Switzerland. Here, we went in a cable car to the top of the mountain where we were able to visit the weather station and get a meal in the café there. We then went on to visit another town on our way back to St. Anton.

The weather for most of the time was dry and sunny and yet it was autumn and the evenings were very chilly.

On our way home we stopped in the black country in Germany at a town called Trebor, which again was built on a very long hill. Here there were many shops selling all kinds of clocks and wood carvings. We wanted to buy an inlaid table but we did not have the right kind of currency to buy it.

We next passed through Salzburg on our way to Nantes where we were to stay for another night before driving to Calais for the ferry. On our arrival in Calais we had to wait for an hour before we could board the ferry. After boarding the ferry, we made for the duty-free shop as soon as we could and we were able to put the bottles of beer in the boot of the coach. However, the driver asked us to bring cigarettes through Customs for him, which we agreed to do, thinking he would give us the receipt. He said it was not needed, but I thought otherwise. We could not leave any bottles of spirits on the coach so we brought them through Customs ourselves. We got through all right but the coach had to go a different way where it was searched. The driver was caught trying to evade Customs Duty on other goods and we were approached by a Customs Officer, where he took the cigarettes and let us off with a warning. We vowed never to do that again when going abroad.

It was early evening before we got back to Worcester, having first stopped for lunch, and dropping people off at Stroud and Gloucester.

We now had to face getting ready for Margaret's birthday, followed by Andrew's, then Christmas, a very busy time for us all.

Chapter Twenty-Three

VERY BAD HEALTH NEWS

We had been invited to the cafe at Callow End to celebrate New Year's Eve and there were about twenty people there. Margaret and I did not know all of them and I was not really interested in what was going on. As soon as it was possible I dropped a hint to Andrew that I thought we ought to take our leave; other people had the same idea. It was very frosty so we had to be careful on the roads coming home.

In April, Margaret and John were asked by the surgery to make appointments for a check-up because neither of them had been to the surgery for years. So, in May, Margaret went one week and John went the following week. Both were given a clean bill of health, except that Margaret did not tell me about the discolouration she had on one of her breasts. Also at this time, the person who had our money invested with his own company and not the one he was working for, told us that the interest from the previous year had gone up by a larger rate than any bank or building society. I could not understand this, so I suggested that we transfer some of our money to other investments with other companies. However, this man persuaded us to leave things as they were and review the position at the end of the year. Margaret, John, Kenneth and I had most of our money tied up with this person and quite thought everything was above board; there seemed to be no need to worry at this time. He hinted that he would like Margaret to cash some of her shares and invest the money with him, but I made a sign to Margaret not to, and wait until later in the year. A few weeks later he turned up on the doorstep and gave me a box containing a bottle of port and Stilton cheese, and asked me to see his new car which, he said, cost him £12,500. I remarked that his business must be doing all right.

We had booked a holiday to Bournemouth for September, but long before that, John and Andrew had booked a holiday in Scotland. They were going to drive up in Andrew's car in June leaving here at 6.00 a.m.. They were going to stay and make Dingwall their base at a hotel there; they got there after a twelve hour drive, sharing the driving. They made many stops on the way because they had never done any long distance driving before. They travelled extensively while they were there and took in several visits to distilleries. At the end of their two weeks' holiday, they arrived home about 1.00 a.m. and when they unloaded the car, they had about a dozen bottles of various malt whiskeys among other souvenirs.

Margaret and I left on a Saturday morning in mid-September by coach to go to Bournemouth. I knew several of the people we were going with and we had a courier with us and we all seemed to have caught the holiday spirit. The hotel was quite close to the sea front, but there was also a bus service from outside which I used while Margaret walked down to the town centre.

We went to Compton Gardens, about two miles from Bournemouth, passing by many houses owned by well-known celebrities, which were pointed out to us by the coach driver. Another trip we did was to catch the ferry and go across the bay to Poole and see some of the sailing ships of previous centuries. We had another coach day trip into the New Forest, where we came in contact with the donkeys and saw the horses and ponies. In one town, there was a shop selling only items for Christmas, from Christmas outfits down to the smallest decorations; it was jammed full and we came away with a calendar for the next year.

One evening when we were changing, getting ready for dinner, I noticed Margaret had one breast which was badly discoloured and I asked her how long it had been like that. I was devastated when she said it had been on and off like that since the medical in May. I told here that on getting home, she was to see the doctor right away, and in any case, why had the nurse not referred her to the doctor in May? Margaret replied, "The nurse and I thought it could be the menopause, and I have to go and stay with mother while Daddy goes off on one of his train journeys when we get back." I said, "No, you see the doctor first." She refused and went to stay with her mother, and promised to see the doctor on her return. I was worried to the extreme because I knew in my own mind what it could possibly be. She saw the doctor in late-October and was referred to a consultant within a week. He diagnosed breast cancer and she would be admitted to hospital on November 6th.

While this was going on, I had tried to contact the man who had all our money. I had recently paid for a new TV set and I wanted to boost up my bank account again. He came to see us two days before Margaret went into hospital. He assured us that the money was safe, but I insisted that he make the arrangements for me to get all our money back to us by the end of the year.

Margaret had her mastectomy operation on 7th November and after ten days or so, she was discharged. She would have to take anti-cancer tablets every day. She had to go to Cheltenham to arrange to have radiotherapy treatment so I went with her. The cancer specialist examined her and marked where the treatment would be, but he also observed that Margaret's other breast was affected; he made a sound to himself but did not make a remark. I noticed this sound but I did not mention it to Margaret; she was worried enough as it was. We were away all day and it was long past teatime before we got home. Since earlier that year I had been doing quite a lot more work in the kitchen, preparing meals and baking cakes with advice from Margaret. After the operation we had a council home care lady to help with the housework. She is a lovely lady and Margaret got used to her bright and breezy manner, and they both got on very well together; so much so, that nothing was too much for her in working for Margaret.

Margaret began her treatment once a week in Cheltenham and I did the shopping and getting meals prepared. I had started making things for Christmas and I was getting very tired at the end of each day. I did not let Margaret know how I was feeling, but I tried to encourage John, Andrew and Kenneth to help a lot more.

I had been trying for days to contact the finance man who had our money, but he could not be found. What with Margaret's illness and now this, things were not looking at all good.

Four days before Christmas I developed a very bad nose bleed and as Margaret came in from one of her treatments, I went out of the door and got to the accident and emergency department at the hospital as quickly as I could. I had pads inserted into my nose and I was told to come back after Christmas. I felt bunged up in my nose and I was feeling very miserable. I carried on as much as possible, but by Christmas Day my nose was bleeding again. John drove me to the hospital, leaving Margaret and Andrew to see to the Christmas dinner.

On our return, I was my own worst enemy, the spirit of Christmas, as far as I was concerned, was non-existent. After the dinner and washing up, we sat down to open our presents and watch the Queen's speech. I was glad when the day ended and could get off to bed. I think I must have spoilt it for everyone.

Margaret had one more treatment to have in the New Year and we were hoping that would be the end of it and that the cancer had gone.

Chapter Twenty-Four

1992

On the 2nd of January, I went to the office of the finance man, only to find the office closed and that the police were looking for him as well as many of his clients like myself. All his mail had been confiscated by the police, and I was advised to contact them by a receptionist in the main office building. I contacted the police who put me in contact with the Fraud Squad. You can imagine how we were all feeling after that news, very worried that we might have lost all our investments. I also had to contact a solicitor in Birmingham who was representing about five other clients. Coupled with this, I had to contact the head office of the insurance company that employed him and also the special investigating board in London.

From now on I was going to be very busy with all this work and to take care of Margaret at the same time.

When Margaret returned from Cheltenham all the signs were that she had made very good progress, but she was referred to the specialist in Worcester again. In late-January I went with Margaret to see him and he said that although everything seemed all right on the one side, the other breast was now affected and needed to be removed. We were both devastated at this news and Margaret almost collapsed with the shock of it. I managed to get her home and a cancer counsellor came to see her.

By now, Margaret was in a terrible state and kept on saying,

"Why me? Why have I got to go through all that again? What have I done to deserve this, and why must I die before my parents?" We all tried to console her and it was a long time before she got over the shock of the news, if she ever did.

In February, I took her to the hospital and she was determined to be well enough to be home for my birthday in March. The operation went off all right and it was now up to Margaret to get well as soon as possible. Before we knew of this second operation we had booked to see Penelope Keith in a play in Birmingham in March, and a week's holiday for the last week in March to go to Sidmouth; so that was something for Margaret to look forward to. Also, we were booked to go to Kleve in Germany with the Swan Theatre Company at the end of May to put on "A Man for All Seasons", after the production here.

This time, Margaret's recovery was much slower than she would have liked and I could see that she might not be home for my birthday. As it turned out, I had made a birthday sponge cake and on my birthday, I got to the hospital as early as I could, taking the cake with me. I was determined to be as cheerful as I could for Margaret, but we both got emotional during my visit. We sat on her bed together having a piece of cake with a cup of tea. John, Andrew and Kenneth came in as they left work and we stayed with Margaret until the end of visiting time at 9.00 p.m..

We were due to go to Birmingham two days later on the Thursday, but it still looked doubtful. When I saw Margaret the next day she was very upset about not going to Birmingham and she was waiting to see the specialist. He said that he saw no reason why she should not go, so it was arranged that we would take her home on Thursday and she could stay at home overnight and return the next day to the ward. We did go to see Penelope Keith and we both enjoyed the play very much, so much so that Margaret was able for a few hours to forget all about what she had been through the past three months. She still had drainage tubes attached to her chest and the bottle was strapped to her middle.

Next morning, Andrew took us back to the ward where I left Margaret, promising to see her again that afternoon. At lunchtime, she phoned me to say that she could come home that day, so John and I went to the hospital and brought her home in time for tea.

Two weeks later, we set off for Sidmouth by coach from here and we picked up more people in Malvern. Margaret was subdued for the first part of the journey and this was noticed by some of the other people. I told them not to say anything to Margaret and I hoped she would be all right when we got to Sidmouth. We arrived in Sidmouth in the late afternoon and settled into our room. We had been given a front room with a small balcony overlooking the sea front. This cheered Margaret up because she loved the sea. We had a cocktail reception at 6.30 p.m. followed by dinner and by now, Margaret was feeling better.

That evening, we all sat around a table and played "Chase the Ace", and both Margaret and I won a game. Margaret was being her old self once again and our party did their best to make sure that Margaret would enjoy herself.

We went for walks along the sea front each day and I was surprised when, on Monday morning, Margaret decided to go for a walk before breakfast on her own. From then on, every evening and morning she did this and by the end of the week, I could see a great change for the better in her.

We had a day trip to Widdicombe-in-the-Moor, which included Dartmeet and Princetown. On another day trip we went to Lyme Regis, Seaton and Beer. The next day we went to Exeter and I took Margaret to see the Cathedral.

We went to the local theatre to see a play one evening, and at the end we were surprised to see the leading male step forward to thank us for coming and being such a good audience.

We arrived back home on the Saturday and John, Andrew and Kenneth could see that the holiday had done Margaret a power of good.

Before going to Sidmouth I had booked seats for Margaret and I to see the Bach Choir sing St Matthew's Passion, at the Symphony Hall in Birmingham on Good Friday. The performance was excellent and we both enjoyed it very much.

The Fraud Squad came to see us on a regular basis, drawing up a dossier on this fraudster of a man. I had to submit copies of the relevant paperwork to them, the solicitor and insurance company.

We were also getting prepared to put on the play "A Man for All Seasons" which was due to start early in May.

The police put out a plea on the B.B.C. Crimewatch U.K. for any sightings of the fraudster and he was arrested late that same evening from a house in Evesham. He was interviewed by the detectives and Fraud Squad for four days and released on bail to appear in court at a later date. He at first denied the charges laid in front of him, until some of the information of his fraud was read out to him; then he admitted the offences. There was so much information to be gathered that we were warned that it would be at least a year before he would be taken to court.

In the meantime, I was in almost weekly contact with the solicitor in Birmingham who was trying to get our money from the insurance company that the man once worked for. All our dealings with him over the years took place in his office of the insurance company. Unknown to us, he was breaking a signed agreement that he would not carry out his private work on their premises.

At about this time also our production manager had developed a cancerous growth on his neck and he was not well. He had received treatment on his neck and the growth was reduced and he had to give up working on the play "A Man for All Seasons". This play was performed early in May for nine nights at the Swan Theatre, and after a week's break, it was time to take the play to Kleve in Germany.

Very early on the Monday we packed the set and costumes in the trailer attached to the rear of the coach and we set off at 7.00 a.m. to get to Dover by 12.00 noon. We all had front seats in the coach, so I sat with Margaret and John and Andrew were opposite us. We got to Dover in good time and got on the ferry by 1.30 p.m. and went for a meal in the café. On arrival in Dieppe we then made our way north towards the Belgian border. The roads were very busy, but we hoped to get to Kleve by early evening. Margaret stood up to the travelling very well and we all thought, at last, she was beginning to look and be her old self again.

On arrival in Kleve we had to meet the people who were going to put us up in their homes. We were placed with a couple about our own age and John and Andrew were with a younger person in another part of Kleve.

The next day we went to the school where we were to perform the play. Margaret was in charge of the costumes backstage, John was stage manager and in charge of the lighting, and Andrew was a member of the cast and backstage crew. I was front-of-house manager, and I had a lad from our group who spoke German fluently as a steward, so that was a great help to me.

We did three performances in all over two days which left us time to be entertained by our respective hosts. Ours took us for sightseeing trips all over Kleve and the surrounding countryside, which included the River Rhine and the Allied Forces' cemetery on the outskirts of Kleve. This, to me, was an emotional experience because most of the men were of my age and generation, and I pointed out to Margaret the West Country names that I recognised on the grave stones. Most of the dead were as a result of the raid on Arnhem which went terribly wrong for the Allies in the 1939-45 War. We signed the visitors' book and Margaret remarked in it that it was a moving experience for us both.

We were also entertained by the Burgomeister in the Rathous one morning for coffee and a brief talk, and we were also entertained one evening. John and Andrew were invited for the evening with us at the house we stayed at, and this was in return for a meal that we had had at the house where John and Andrew stayed.

My realisation from all this was that we may have won the War, but Germany had certainly won the peace.

Since the War ended Kleve had been mostly rebuilt including its hospital and ancient castle, and the car parks were built underground. The house we stayed at had a kitchen, dining room, bathroom and lounge converted to a bedroom downstairs for us, and upstairs, except for the kitchen, was repeated over again even to the dining room suite.

* * * *

We returned home in early June and we arrived about 3.00 a.m. because of the hold-ups on the Continent making us late. It began to rain later on and when I went downstairs about 9.00

a.m., I discovered a leak in the bay window where it joined the main part of the building. The next day I set about getting a builder to survey the damage and he said that we needed a new roof on the bay window. We finished up by having that repaired and covered in lead, and having the whole outside of the house repainted, and a new solid front door fitted.

In the back garden, we found that the raspberries were just ready to start picking, so Margaret and I set about gathering them each day.

We had been home about two days when Margaret complained about her chest itching and I asked her to let me see it. When I looked at it, it was as red as a beetroot; she had also caught a cold. The next day I took her to see the nurse first and she referred her to the doctor right away. He gave her some tablets for her cold and asked her how soon would she be going to Cheltenham for a check-up, and she said in two weeks' time.

The next week we went on a trip on the River Severn from Stourport. She was not feeling too good, although it was a warm and pleasant day. She felt that if she did not go, she would be letting me down, and when we arrived home she went to bed. This was to be the last time that a photo of her was taken. She never complained about how she felt at any time, but I could see a change in her which I did not like.

I insisted on going to the Cheltenham hospital with her and we saw the specialist again. He told Margaret that the rash on her chest was more cancer, and that her only chance was a course of chemotherapy. At that time she was having difficulty breathing and she insisted on being admitted to a ward to have her treatment. It was touch and go whether the treatment would work and she was told this. She then asked, "How long have I got?" and the reply staggered me, let alone Margaret. It would be lucky if she survived this side of Christmas.

Margaret was kept in and I came home, not knowing when I would see her again. I waited until all the men had come home from work and I told them as much as I dare at that time. I don't think that they realised how ill Margaret was. I was getting very frustrated not knowing what to do. I decided to phone the hospital to find out how Margaret was and I was told that the visiting hours were from 9.00 a.m. until 9.00 p.m.. With that, I said to the men, "Come on, let's all get in the car and go and see your Mum." So we locked up the house and drove to Cheltenham, getting there between 6.00 and 7.00 p.m.. Margaret was in bed resting and nothing had been done for her up to then. I went in search of the sister or senior nurse on duty to find out what and when Margaret would get anything done to ease her breathing. She had been given the chemotherapy by injection in her arm and she would get the rest in four-weekly intervals. The specialist was due to see Margaret that evening or the next morning. By the time we returned on Saturday afternoon they had drained some fluid from her chest and she was feeling a little better. The next day I was informed by the ward sister that Margaret could come home on Monday if she had improved further.

A school teacher friend of ours offered her car at my disposal to run round for Margaret while the three men were all at work during the day. We had been given an answerphone by them as a wedding anniversary present; so this friend and I set it up and then we went to Cheltenham in the hope that we would be able to bring Margaret home. We had to wait quite some time before the specialist came to examine Margaret and afterwards have a private word with me. He warned me in no uncertain terms, confirming what he'd said to Margaret on the previous Friday, that she might not get over this illness and that she might not see Christmas or the New Year. I had to keep this information to myself, but one look at me and Margaret could guess that the news was not good.

We arrived home in time for tea, and everyone was glad to see Margaret home again. By the next day, Margaret's breathing was difficult again and when the nurse came to see her, she advised us that she would send for the doctor the next day if there was no improvement. The nurse arrived early the next morning and sent for the doctor immediately. After he'd examined Margaret, he phoned for an ambulance and within minutes, one arrived. Kenneth had also arrived, being sent home from work as soon as the doctor had phoned. He followed us to the hospital in his car and met us there.

He and I had to wait a long time before we were able to see Margaret and once we saw that she was more settled, we left to get a meal and to phone John and Andrew. After visiting time that evening a drainage tube was inserted into Margaret's back and, overnight, about four to five pints of fluid was drained off. After this, she was able to breathe a lot better and after a further six days in hospital, we were able to bring her home.

News from the solicitor was much better. We were informed that the insurance company was prepared to pay us the money in full that had been stolen from us by the fraudster. This was very good news from our point of view, but we also realised a number of his clients were not going to be so lucky. At the end of August we did get all our money repaid to us, so, we were fully solvent again.

Margaret continued her visits to Cheltenham for chemotherapy and I could see a marked difference in her that she looked very tired, and she began to spend more time in bed in the mornings.

Now we were advised to have the house rewired to meet the Common Market standards. We had been recommended to an electrician and we set a date in September to have the house rewired in two days at a weekend.

Up to then we had not celebrated Kenneth's twenty-first birthday in April, nor our wedding anniversary and John's birthday in August. We agreed to go out for a meal early in September one weekend soon after Margaret came home from hospital and before the rewiring was done.

Soon after this Margaret felt well enough to go out shopping one day on her own. Kenneth took her by car as far as the High Street and arranged to collect her from there a little later. The next week we all went to a trading estate to get some new light fittings and shades, which we let Margaret choose. We had the home help three times a week, an hour each time, so this was a help to us.

The nurse still called each morning and I could get one from the hospital at night if needed.

The electrician came on the Saturday midway through the month and stripped out all the old wiring that day very quickly. On the Sunday, Andrew took Margaret out to the café at Callow

End so that she would not tire herself with all the noise of the men. By the evening, we were back to normal with everything working and we all went out to Callow End to bring Margaret home. She managed to go for a fair good walk while she had been out there.

Margaret's breathing had become difficult again and she was readmitted into hospital to have her lungs drained once more. She was in hospital for a further ten days and she came home towards the end of September. On her return she made me promise not to let her be taken back into hospital again. She had asked me this in front of the senior district nurse, so we both promised her that her wish would be granted.

By this time Margaret was wearing a wig because of the loss of her hair and soon after she returned home, her brother, Hugh, and his daughter, Allison, came to see her from St. Albans. They had travelled by train and they could only stay just a few hours before returning home again.

Members of St. Richard's Hospice close by here came in most days to sit with Margaret while I went out to do the shopping. They were a great help to Margaret and saw to her needs, and they even put the laundry in the washing machine for me. This became a very busy household, all for Margaret's needs. Each day we had the nurses calling twice and sometimes three times a day. Then we had the doctors calling almost daily, then the home help and the people from the Hospice, and of course John, Andrew and Kenneth coming and going to work.

We had booked to see an ice show, featuring Torville and Dean, at the Indoor Arena in Birmingham, for mid-October. I was determined that Margaret, if possible, would not miss it. She looked forward to this trip very much and we had a lovely evening at the ice show, but Margaret had become very slow in walking, so she had to rely on me in helping her. The steps were very steep inside the arena so we took our time getting to our seats. Margaret really enjoyed herself that night and was delighted with the skating exhibition that we saw.

We went together for her next chemotherapy treatment and our friend, Nigel, was also going for treatment on his neck and staying in the hospital for more tests for a few days.

Each morning I would take Margaret her breakfast of cornflakes, toast and marmalade, and a cup of tea. I called her Lady Penelope and myself Parker, which are two characters from Thunderbirds, the TV programme. This was to cheer her up and try to stop her getting depressed and for the most part, it worked. After this I would help her to the bathroom and help her to wash if she needed my help. Since the end of August I had been helping Margaret in getting dressed, and it became a normal everyday occurrence from then on, until the nurses decided it was better for them to help Margaret; their visits were now twice a day. This left me free to do all the shopping, and preparing and cooking the meals.

Olive brought her parents to see Margaret and if they were shocked at seeing Margaret, they did not show it or remark on it. As Margaret watched them leave from the bay window, she said to me, "That's the last time that I will see Mum and Dad." I said, "Don't be silly, when you are better again, you can go and see them."

After this visit from her parents she showed signs of getting weaker, especially with walking and standing, so I helped her each time she wanted to move. She was taking several kinds of drugs each day, and I think that was worse than the chemotherapy, and now I had to help her into and out of the bed. Where I got the strength to do this, I never knew, but it must have come from somewhere.

Early on the Monday evening a week after her parents had been to see her, she announced that she was going to bed, so I helped her up the stairs and got her into bed. I stayed with her for a while and then she wanted to have a sleep. When I went to bed that night I took her a warm drink which she had and then settled down to sleep, but she had a bad night with very little sleep. The next morning when the nurse arrived, she suggested that Margaret would get a better night if I slept downstairs. We managed to borrow a single bed which we put in the front room for me.

Margaret began to get worse as each day passed and on the next Saturday, her sister, Olive, phoned from Bath and asked if she could come and see Margaret. She agreed to this and Olive and her friend Betty arrived in mid-afternoon. They stayed to tea and left about 7.00 p.m. to return to Calne. It was now Sunday 1st November and Margaret's birthday would be on Wednesday, the 4th, so we had hoped to make it a good one for her. She had stopped having a proper breakfast about three weeks before and she was just having mostly liquids and all the drugs that she was taking. She had now been in bed for two weeks.

On the Monday, the senior nurse came at teatime to have a talk to all four of us. She ushered us into the front room and went to the kitchen and made a pot of tea and brought it in to us. She then told us that she and the doctors did not think that Margaret would live very much longer, perhaps a week or ten days at the most. This really knocked us sideways. Yes, I knew that we could lose Margaret, but on the other hand, John, Andrew and Kenneth found it difficult to come to terms with this news. They all asked wasn't there any more that could be done to save her, but the answer was still, "No."

A night nurse came to sit with Margaret for two nights that week to give me a rest from taking care of her, but Margaret had little or no sleep each time. I did not sleep any better myself either with worrying about her.

On Wednesday we had three large bouquets of flowers arrive for Margaret, one was from me, and another from Bruce and Celia, and the third from the Children's Theatre at the Swan. She also had many cards from friends and relations. The bedroom was like a florist's shop and Margaret was overwhelmed by it. I did not make her a cake nor did I mention it but I did give her a bed jacket which the nurses dressed her in after seeing to her wash and other needs.

The vicar was asked to call and see us as he had been warned that Margaret was terminally ill. It was arranged that Margaret would take Holy Communion the next day if she was well enough. She had also, unknown to me, been picking out the hymns for her funeral which she discussed with the vicar. With his help, and mine to a lesser degree, she arranged everything for the service. This was very depressing and I got very emotional about it because I did not want to lose her. She was to me my sweetheart, wife, and best friend, all rolled into one, and I knew that I would be lost without her.

On Thursday 5th November we took Communion together in the afternoon.

Friday was a very busy day for me and we had someone in to sit with Margaret while I went out to do the shopping. While I was out I met two ladies that we both knew, one whom I had worked with and the other was a member of the Theatre staff. They both asked about Margaret and were sorry to hear she was not at all well.

When John arrived home from work the lady from St. Richard's who was here suggested that he make us all a cup of tea. This he did without question and he was told that I had done more than my share of work that day, which included getting the laundry washed and dried.

On the next day I had arranged for the small TV to be fitted in the bedroom so that Margaret could watch the TV if she wanted to. This entailed drilling a hole in the wall for the aerial cable, and more holes in the chimney breast for the TV bracket. It did not bother Margaret at all and she was able to say exactly where the TV shelf should go on the wall.

It was Children's Theatre this morning and John and Andrew had gone to help, and Margaret remarked to me, "I wonder how the play is going today?" I replied by saying that no doubt John and Andrew would tell us when they came home. Even though she was so ill, she was still thinking of other people, which was typical of her. When John and Andrew came home, Margaret wanted to know who was there and how did the play go.

That evening, we watched TV together until Margaret had a visit from the nurse. She had come to settle Margaret for the night. For some unknown reason, she asked me to sleep with her that night, which I did. On her side of the bed she was supported by a water mattress which made her higher in the bed than me. On reflection, did she have a premonition about the next day? Since then I have often wondered about that.

She did not have a good night being awake most of the time and when I awoke, she asked me to get her a cup of tea, and to make sure that I did not get cold in doing so, again thinking of me and not herself. This was sometime between 4.00 and 5.00 a.m.. Then, much later on, she asked me, "What time is it?" I checked the clock and I said that it was 7.30 a.m.. Then she asked me, "What day is it?" When I said, "Don't you know?", she replied, "No, and I can't hear the boys getting up for work." I then told her it was Sunday. With that, she said, "Good, so everyone is at home today," and I said, "Yes." This reply was also a puzzle to me.

Later, after my breakfast, she began to worry about the nurse coming in to see to her wash etc. and I had to stay with her until the nurse came. I noticed at times she seemed to be drifting into unconsciousness.

On this visit two nurses came and after they both went upstairs to see to Margaret, one of them came down into the kitchen and warned us that Margaret might not last the day. I was preparing lunch with help from John and Andrew and as it was about 11.00 a.m., someone decided to make us all a cup of coffee.

After lunch, Kenneth went out for a drive in his car but he was home again after an hour. Margaret had begun to lose consciousness, so we had sent for the doctor and after he had seen Margaret, he asked me to see him in the dining room. He said that Margaret might not last the night so we must be prepared for the worst.

He left us and I stayed with Margaret while the boys watched the TV downstairs. John brought me a cup of tea at teatime and Margaret said to him, "Go on downstairs, John, I'll be all right, Dad is with me." So John then went back to the dining room. I sat on the bed beside Margaret and when, much later, the phone rang it was Nigel who wanted to know how Margaret was. John told him the latest news, which wasn't good.

Later, at about 6.35 p.m., I said to Margaret, "Do you want to watch 'Songs of Praise'?" and she said, "Yes," so I switched the TV on and as the newsreader signed off, Margaret sat up in bed, gave a shriek from the pain and fell back in the bed again; she had died at that moment at exactly 6.40 p.m..

I called out to the boys and they came rushing up the stairs and I said, "I think Mum has gone. One of you phone for the doctor." Andrew did this, then he phoned for the nurses on duty and by 7.00 p.m., they were all here. The doctor confirmed that Margaret was dead. Before the nurses laid her out they asked me if there was anything special to be buried with her, and I said, "Yes there is, you can dress her in her nightdress from her sister and put her bedjacket on," which I had given to her for her birthday only four days before. We also wrapped up a group family photo and placed it in her hands.

The vicar arrived after Evensong and while he was here, the undertaker came and removed Margaret to the chapel of rest. When the vicar asked me how long had we been married, I said without thinking, "Thirty-two years, two months, two days and seven hours forty minutes." I was amazed at my reply so I could only put it down to initial shock and reaction.

After the vicar left I phoned Bruce, who had been phoning very often for news, and told him the bad news. I asked him would he still come and stay on Tuesday for two or three days. He phoned Ron for me and then I phoned Olive. She in turn told her parents.

I could not believe that Margaret had gone and the more I thought about the past year, I realised that she had the first operation on November 7th and precisely one year and one day later, she had died.

Bruce arrived by train on the Tuesday and he stayed at a local hotel nearby for three nights. I was glad of this because he was able to support me and he helped me to choose an overcoat that I needed. He went home to Spalding and came back three days later with Stephen and his wife Heather, by car, and he, Ron and Joyce stayed at the hotel overnight. We had delayed the funeral until 17th November so that the funeral arrangements could be finalised and to enable most relatives and friends to attend.

On arriving at the church I was quite surprised to see so many people there which were mostly friends, although we had very good support from both sides of the family. After the internment, we came home and we had our friends from the café at Callow End, who did a good job with the catering. I know that Margaret's parents were very surprised at the number of people who knew her and came to the service.

Two days later we all went to the cemetery to take photos of the grave and each time that I went there, I got more upset, so I began to cut down on my visits.

A counsellor from St. Richard's Hospice started to visit me to counsel me, but she made me feel more upset than I needed to be. In the end, I asked her not to call any more because I was getting worse rather than better, and I began to improve much more when her visits ceased.

Our next problem was how were we to manage from now on. There was the housework to think about with cleaning and laundry and ironing, which I could not do, but I could manage most of the shopping and cooking.

At first, the cooking was a hit and miss type of thing, but with trial and error experience, I began to put on fairly good meals. The kitchen units were all in a bad condition with some of them nearly falling off the walls, so I decided that we needed new units fitted. In the end, we had the kitchen redesigned and it was arranged that the work would be started in January.

Having the kitchen to think about took the loss of Margaret off our minds for a while. As Christmas was not far away, I was dreading it.

With the anniversary of the death of my Mother on 22nd December in 1977 and recently losing Margaret, it was not going to be a happy time at all for us. We just went through the motions of Christmas and New Year from the food point of view, but we were glad when the season was over. I was still in a daze and trying to come to terms with my great loss. I was hoping that the New Year would, in some respects, be a better one.

Chapter Twenty-Five

A NEW YEAR & A NEW BEGINNING

Early in January 1993 the workmen arrived to start work on the kitchen. This was going to take eight working days to complete and unlike when the extension was built, it was completed in the given time.

We now had an electric double oven and separate to that, we had a gas hob fitted, and we had more cupboard space than we had ever had in the past. I placed a photo of Margaret in the kitchen and I named it "Margaret's Kitchen". That was because she had left me the money to pay for it.

It was shortly after this that Margaret's Uncle Raymond died aged ninety-three, but we were unable to go to the funeral.

At home, the housework was not being done to my satisfaction and I was getting more frustrated as time went by in having to do most, if not all, of it myself. It got so bad that, in desperation, I phoned Bruce and asked him if I could come and stay with him for a few days. I felt that I needed to get away from here, and the sooner the better. When Andrew, John and Kenneth came home from work, I made them all sit down as I had something to say.

I told them that I was not satisfied with the way things were and that I was not to be taken for granted anymore, and expect me to wait on them. We came to a compromise where I would do the cooking, and they in turn were expected to clear away and do the washing up. Then, if they were not to take it in turns with the ironing, they could do their own. I also said that I would still do most of the shopping, but that I expected them to get the heavy and bulky goods. I then told them that I was going away and I did not know when I would be back, but when I did, I expected to find the house clean and tidy when I returned. They then asked me where I was going so I told them that I was going to stay with Uncle Bruce.

The next day, I left and went by train to Peterborough where Bruce and Celia met me and we stopped for a snack lunch on our way to Spalding. I stayed a week in which time Bruce and I went to the snooker club a couple of times and we did a shopping trip to Peterborough. We also went to see Stephen and Heather on the Sunday, where we had lunch. I gave them presents before I left and I returned home to Worcester. The house had been cleaned but not fully, there were still some areas that needed attention.

In May, the trial was held in Hereford of the fraudster. I went to the court to see what the outcome would be. He had embezzled roughly £250,000 in total, involving about twenty or more people. When he entered the court room, that was the first time that I had seen him since early in November 1991. He was sentenced to three years imprisonment which I thought was far too lenient, and I have not seen him since. After eighteen months he was released from prison, a free man again. I can only hope that one day the insurance company will catch up with him and make his life hell.

As Margaret did most of the gardening, I decided that as John, Andrew and Kenneth had never had an interest nor helped very much in the past, I would have a patio built with Cotswold stone brick walls surrounding it. I had my ideas put to a plan and I finished up not with one, but two patios and a barbecue fitted, one patio being built higher with a different stone design covering it.

This cut out most of the gardening, but it was me that still did what needed to be done. I tried to cut the work down to the minimum by having certain plants that needed very little attention.

Our friend Nigel died in June from cancer, and Margaret's mother died early in July from an internal haemorrhage, aged ninety-four. We attended the funeral, but what a lot of people noticed was no mention of Margaret in the eulogy of the family. Quite a lot was said about her brother Frank, who died at a very early age in Persia. I was really upset by this and I mentioned it to Olive, who also had noticed it.

I had booked a holiday to the Lake District, which was to be my first one without Margaret, and I was a little apprehensive when the day came to go. I need not have worried about that, because Gay, the courier, who had known Margaret, made sure that I would enjoy myself. I really did enjoy it, but there were many times during the week that I still missed Margaret being with me.

Another friend who knew Margaret was Beryl and she had the knack of making me laugh quite a lot; she put me at my ease most of the time. We had such a rapport that to the others, we seemed to be always joking with each other. As a thank you I gave Beryl a large box of chocolates on the night before we came home.

I had noticed that the housework was still being a chore for all of us, so again I told all three that if they were not prepared to do it between them, I would have to find a woman to come and do the work and that they would have to pay the woman for the work. These women are hard to find, but after I had advertised, I managed to get a lady to come in and do the ironing and house cleaning two mornings a week, which took a load off my mind.

I now began to socialise more, going out to the theatres a lot, not only here in Worcester but also to London, Birmingham and Bristol. From now on, I hoped that the future would be brighter for me, but I still ask the question, as Margaret did, "Why me, why have I been left to face the future alone without the most precious person that Margaret was and meant to me?" I shall never forget that last Sunday when we lost her, nor will I ever forget her who, after all, has been constantly in my thoughts ever since the first day that I met her, and she still is.

Plymouth Library

Treasured
Loving Memories Of
My Darling Sweetheart Wife
MARGARET FRANCES
DUNKLEY
BORN 4TH NOVEMBER 1936.
PASSED INTO GOD'S KEEPING
8TH NOVEMBER 1992.
AGED 56 YEARS
Till We Meet Again

You Are Now And Always Will Be
Greatly Missed